After her early life with her endlessly restless mother, Sarah became a documentary maker for Channel 4 and the BBC. Her films have taken her on several trips around India and the US, across Mexico and up the Nile, and back to some of the places she visited with Audrey decades before. After building a cabin on a secluded beach she finally managed to settle enough to write this memoir, and is currently working on her next book, a novel. She has four children and lives with her partner in London and the south coast.

Praise for *Diamonds at the Lost and Found*:

'Aspinall's wealth of narrative gifts are on display throughout this engrossing memoir. On the spider's web of fragile – and fragmented – childhood memories and half-understood snatches of conversation, Aspinall brings her late mother to life again'   *Irish Times*

'A great read – what a strange and amazing life! The tone was pitched just right, unflinchingly, but with so much love and after reading it I felt that maybe I understood something more about the world of women'   LOUIS THEROUX

'Wry and warm: I went from gripped to moved and tearful and I'd now like to read a hundred more books by this ~~if~~ d. vivid storyteller'   MARIAN

'It's a story of how a mother passes onto her daughter the greatest gift of all – a passion for life! Like everyone who reads it I wish I had met Audrey just once!'   JOHN BISHOP

'Everyone has a mother but not everyone's mother is like Audrey. I found myself completely immersed in the incredibly vivid world of this memoir and was sad to leave it behind'   KATE ATKINSON, author of *Big Sky*

'Aspinall elevates her familial memories from the personal into something more: a kind of social history, taking in grey, post-war Britain, Technicolor America, the Swinging Sixties and seedy Seventies. A documentary-maker, she injects the book with a cinematic quality'   *The Times*

'A remarkable memoir of a one-off childhood where the normal rules do not apply, with unforgettable characters and exotic locations a-plenty, and where glamour, adventure and being invited to the party are all that matters'
CATHERINE SIMPSON, author of *When I Had a Little Sister*

'Exciting tales of an electrifying yet altruistic woman . . . a terrific memoir'   *Readers Digest*

Diamonds
at the
Lost and Found

A Memoir in Search of my Mother

SARAH ASPINALL

4th Estate • London

4th Estate
An imprint of HarperCollins*Publishers*
1 London Bridge Street
London SE1 9GF

www.4thEstate.co.uk

HarperCollins*Publishers*
1st Floor, Watermarque Building, Ringsend Road
Dublin 4, Ireland

First published in Great Britain in 2020 by 4th Estate
This 4th Estate paperback edition published in 2021

1

A catalogue record for this book is available from the British Library

ISBN 978-0-00-837519-5

Image on page 108 © Everett Collection Inc/Alamy Stock Photo
Image on page 183 © Pictorial Press Ltd/Alamy Stock Photo
All other images provided by the author.

Set in Adobe Garamond Pro

Printed and bound by CPI Group (UK) Ltd, Croydon

MIX
Paper from
responsible sources
FSC
www.fsc.org
FSC™ C007454

This book is produced from independently certified FSC paper
to ensure responsible forest management

Find out more about HarperCollins and the environment at
www.harpercollins.co.uk/green

To Molly

Contents

I

Hong Kong

I AM EIGHT YEARS OLD and it is 1965.

I look around the softly lit bar. A man sits across from me on a high stool, well dressed, alone, drink in hand; I notice him straight away. The air is smoky and the distant lights glittering below us could be those of Tokyo or Cairo or San Francisco, or any of these cities that we find ourselves in. The glitzy decor, rich smells and leather dinner menus give no clues as to even what country we are in, only what level we are currently at in International Hotel Land. This week it is Hong Kong, the hotel sumptuous, and we are hopeful this may be one of our winning streaks.

'*I've got you under my skin . . .*'

A pianist is playing Sinatra songs. He drifts seamlessly from one to the next –

'*. . . In the wee small hours of the morning . . .*'

I know the songs; they play everywhere we go and my mother sings along to them all.

In the hotel lobby is a Chinese emperor's throne that you can sit on to be photographed. A kindly American couple takes a picture of me sitting on it, lifting me onto the scarlet cushion, putting the Mandarin hat with tassels on my head and telling me to smile. They scribble down the address that my mother gives them, promising to mail a print of it to my 'home'.

I keep thinking about this, and wondering if one day we will go to a place called home. Will this photograph be waiting for me, lying on a doormat in an envelope with an American stamp? I try to picture 'home', and to remember the gloomy tiled hallway in the big Victorian house in the damp seaside town, but it only feels like somewhere that I've once visited, and not much liked.

Tonight we eat dinner in the dining room off the lobby and bar, and for once my mother can find little to say. Around us is the usual hotel mix of tanned tourist families and businessmen having serious conversations, or off duty with a beer, chatting about golf. I'm not allowed to read my books at mealtimes, so I look around the room trying to find something to be interested in.

'... *do be do* ... *the lady is a tramp* ...' The pianist drawls, Audrey joins in.

'Why is she a tramp?' I ask.

'She wants to be free, do her own thing,' she says, 'you know,' then she croons about having the wind in our hair and being without a care. As she sings she does the thing she calls table jiving, her hands criss-crossing through the air, fists thumping each other, thumbs pointing over her shoulder as if she was hitch-hiking right out of the restaurant.

'So why won't she go there in erming and pearls? What is erming?'

She sighs. 'It's ermine, min, fur, you know like my mink coat.'

She doesn't like these sorts of questions. Sometimes she will give me a number, like 'OK, three, two more', and hold three fingers up, taking each finger down as I ask her something.

She takes out one of her menthol cigarettes and smokes it slowly, then tries to be kind.

'Have an ice cream, sweetheart? You've hardly eaten anything.'

But I don't want an ice cream and I feel sick. I know she is bored, and I shouldn't ask anything else.

'Shall I get myself a *Coke* then?' I offer. Audrey looks over at the bar again, at the man sitting there.

'OK then.'

This is code and we both know what is going to happen next.

I get up and make my way across to the bar; I manage to wedge myself right next to the man sitting on his stool and I can feel the rough cloth of his jacket against my arm and smell that faint male smell of aftershave and car leather and five-pound notes. The waiter fills my glass with ice and I turn to the man with what I hope is a cute smile.

'Hello.'

He looks down at me from his bar stool. 'Hello, princess.'

I give him an innocent look. 'I don't suppose you can look after my Mummy when I go to bed?'

He seems taken aback, but then laughs and turns to glance behind him. 'So which one is your mummy? And are you quite sure she wants to be taken care of?'

I nod and point across to her. Audrey gives a puzzled smile as she gets up to come over, pretending she doesn't know what is happening. She transforms herself in those few moments, into someone happy and fascinating.

'Oh dear, is my little girl being a pest?' she says, and puts her arm around me.

She has a voice that sounds excited and drowsy at the same time, and an accent she has invented for herself, a trace of her parents' Irish Liverpool mixed with something faintly American. People are intrigued and ask her, they always do . . . 'Where do you come from?'

Now with the man there is that sudden shift, a change in the atmosphere, and in him. He suddenly looks younger and more alive as he takes in the strands of red hair that fall across her face, the look she has, bright-eyed and as if there was some joke going on that no one else knew about, a joke just between them. It makes a room feel like the chandeliers have just been lit and everything sparkles.

He responds as they so often do, with that look of keen, warm interest. 'This little princess was just telling me that she was going to bed?'

I decide then that I don't think he is very nice, not really. I think he might be what my Auntie Grace, who doesn't like my mother, would call 'one of her smooth smoothies'. Audrey gives me what she believes is her motherly look.

'She certainly is off to bed. Come on, Miss Flip!'

4

I get up and say goodnight to my catch of the evening. She is pleased with me. She has a hundred names for me: Miss Doodlemepop is my favourite.

Then, just as we are leaving, he takes the bait as they always do. He leans in towards her.

'Maybe we could have a little nightcap?'

His voice is full of meaning. He smiles down at me.

'So this little lady won't have to worry about Mummy being all alone?'

'Oh I don't know,' she says modestly, thinking about it, wondering if it would be OK. Then, with a 'what the heck' air as if throwing a lifetime of caution to the wind, she gives in.

'It wouldn't hurt, I suppose, just a quick one. I'll settle her down first.'

Back in the room 'settling me down' means that I pull on my nightie, guiltily ignoring the flannel and toothbrush that Auntie Grace had presented me with. She'd been horrified that I'd never had a toothbrush, let alone been told to use one. Then I get into bed to watch the delicious routine of Mummy 'freshening up': the grey-green eyeliner smudged along her eyes, the coral lipstick blotted with a Kleenex, and lastly the squirt of the perfume bottle and the cloud of Youth Dew which she will lightly step into. In that moment I am entranced with her. It is like a special dance, swirling into a haze of fragrance as it curls around her, settling on her hair, her skin, as if a magical dew. Hers is the smell of the fresh early evening, black taxicabs and Martinis, mink coats and diamonds. Sometimes she will let me step into that perfume

5

cloud and I fantasize about what my own grown-up special scent will be. I imagine honeysuckle and bluebell woods, and try to remember what these things smell like. Does England smell this way after summer showers? It should, but all I can remember is the cold sea air and rain on the windows of that sad, faraway house.

She's ready, and there's the feeling of her cheek brushing mine and the click of the door closing behind her. I lie in the dark, listening for the reassuring sounds of other hotel guests running baths and the murmur of conversation. Tonight I feel that she won't be back till morning, but I know she will come back. She always comes back.

I switch the light back on and reach for my book.

The random books I collected as I passed through childhood had become, at this time, my entire guide to life. Bought in haste at airports, found abandoned in hotel lounges or given to me by sympathetic strangers, this odd library system yielded up occasional gold. Some of the content was baffling, or dull, or written in impenetrable language, but I kept going just for those precious moments of illumination when something in the story gave me a key to understanding the strange situations that I found myself in. One current favourite was called *Coffee, Tea or Me?*, which followed air stewardesses Trudy and Rachel as they engaged in a daily battle to ward off the attentions of the airline pilots, drunk passengers and 'love 'em and leave 'em guys' travelling the world. We met a lot of these ladies, who seemed so kind and elegant. We would see them again after our flight, crossing the airport concourse or hotel lobby, as they walked behind the captain

6

and co-pilot, in their trim uniforms. But I now realize that behind that poise was a struggle for survival. A hunt of their own, the same hunt we were on.

Tonight I would struggle on with a book I'd found: *Of Human Bondage* by Somerset Maugham. It begins with the hero Philip as a child, sleeping safe and loved in his mother's arms, and then being told, 'Your mamma's gone away. You won't ever see her any more. Your mamma's in heaven.' The sense of panic and abandonment that he felt is exactly how I had felt at the death of my father. I was still unable to think of his sad, kind face without a frozen sense of misery.

As a guide to how adults love each other this story couldn't be more shocking. Philip has a deformed back, and is terribly sensitive; he falls in love with a waitress called Mildred who is cruel to him, and who he seems to find repellent with her 'common nasal voice', but he cannot think about anything else. Love was my chosen subject of study, and the feelings of Philip for Mildred were so different from any childish idea of love that I felt some trick was being played on the reader.

I didn't want to ask my mother, as she didn't like to talk about things in books. But if a man like Philip could love a horrid girl like Mildred, then why didn't one of those men who my mother met ever love her, when she was so beautiful and could sing and dance and tell funny stories and make the room light up? It must just have been a run of terrible, terrible luck.

Sometimes on our adventures, 'our travels', we were in luck. We could stay in lavish hotels with gorgeous lobbies and mirrored ballrooms, with long corridors and caged lifts:

wonderlands that I could explore for hours. Then we would suddenly lurch into an entirely different world of cheap rooms and panic.

Morning comes, and I wake up with hot light coming through a narrow line down the side of the curtains, cutting across the hotel room. Audrey is sitting in a chair with her wrap around her. She isn't doing anything. Just sitting there.

THIS IS AUDREY.

She looks so small now.

Today she's made up like a doll; I can't get past the likeness. Then I note the empty space in her oversized coffin has been padded with sparkling pink gauze.

A doll in a presentation box.

And yet I look at her now and that strange magnetic aura is still there. The rumble of a bus on the road outside does little to erase it. Otherwise this room is so silent, she is so still, her stories already drifting away from me, some already half forgotten.

I see now that my mother and I lived in a land of these stories. It began back then with my own escape into books, and Audrey's myriad tales told to strangers. Ours was a fairyland of myth and anecdote, sometimes in dull black and white, sometimes Technicolor; always a musical and often a romance. Only once or twice was it a tragedy, but we got over it.

As a child there was this constant swirling mist around us, made up of all these fragments of my mother's past, her thousand and one tales. Many were extraordinary accounts of ingenuity and good fortune, most were true, but even then I believed there was another, untold story, which hovered over us, a story that we were either leaving behind or travelling towards.

I knew, even then, that my mother was many things – a chancer, a dreamer, a procurer, a delinquent, as well as a teller of tales.

Here is one of her tales: Marilyn Monroe's favourite bungalow was Number Seven on the studio backlot, the Norma Jean, which sat behind a dapple of succulent foliage; beyond it a path wound through tropical gardens to Bungalow Four. An assistant was taking room-service sandwiches wrapped in white linen to Clark Gable and another a tray of Martinis to Frank Sinatra in Bungalow Five. Against these tangled depths, shaded by twilight, the flames of bougainvillea match Audrey's lipstick, and a lamp glints off her auburn hair. She has found her way to Oz, and infiltrated the magic kingdom of the movies at last. There is a patter of rain, the sky is darkening and Sinatra steps outside holding a drink – he puts out his hand to catch a raindrop and smiles.

'What do you call a wet bear?' Audrey asks him.

'I don't know.' He grins. 'What do you call a wet bear?'

'A drizzly bear.'

He laughs, and raises his glass to her before moving back into the shadows.

Clink.

This is Audrey.

Crimson lips, salty tears, the sad house and the windy dunes.

Bougainvillea, Sinatra, warm breeze through the Hollywood Hills.

And me here to work out how she and I fit in between.

There's a thread running through our story, our harum-scarum life, and it is love; perhaps, more than that, a *hunt* for love?

The love between a man and a woman was clearly everything. I think back to myself as a child and realize that this was coded into me. All the nooks and crannies, breezes and becalmings, the highs and lows that rattled us over the world and back are somehow connected to that thread.

Love was everything to her. To us. That hunt was everything.

I now see it drove her every day.

My mission is to work out why it took us so long to find it.

It made me who I am, that adventure, and those years of being her small partner in crime. I wasn't always able to see where we were going but, like the back of a pantomime horse, I could hear, and in time I learnt so much. So my own story must now be about what I lost and found along the way.

2

Star Quality

THE SOUTHPORT SEA had receded to a faraway ribbon of silver, and a ghostly view of Blackpool Tower shimmered across the mud and water of the estuary. On autumn nights this mirage would pulsate with light and colour and I was told that it contained a circus with dancing ponies and roaring lions.

Our first house was pebble-dashed and on a dull road of bed-and-breakfast VACANCY signs. The road went down to the so-called seaside, a dark mudflat lit with pools of reflecting water as it stretched into the distance. Silt had slowly filled the bay, and the vanishing sea had already robbed Southport of its life as a genteel resort; but at the end of the 1950s it was still holding on grimly, propping up the old fairground and planting its municipal pleasure grounds with cheery geraniums.

There was a box of cine films in the sideboard at home, labelled in my father's careful handwriting. These were eventually lost in my mother's endless house moves, so it is now hard to be sure what is a memory of life, and what is a memory of these flickering records of my childhood. Both have the same uneven quality, the shifts in luminosity, the haze of things that are glimpsed through gauze. My earliest childhood summers still have, in my mind, that fragile vibrancy of watercolours, and in every frame my mother sparkles. She steps out of shadows and into a transparent glow as if lit from within and fluttering with life, quivering with the next thing she wants or needs.

One flickering recollection is of a hot day in midsummer. We walk down to a seafront teeming with bank-holiday crowds as Mummy holds my hand tightly. The Marine Pleasure Gardens, with their rolling acres of lawns and lakes, are a magic kingdom to me, as we cross mock-Venetian bridges snaking over lagoons thick with chugging pleasure boats. The overhead rollercoaster creaks and explodes with screams. I am lifted up to wave at the miniature railway, rattling by us under the shadow of the pier and out into sunlight and past the cages of rabbits along the route on its way to the zoo.

We approach the high circular wall of the salty Sea Bathing Lake where seawater was still pumped from the distant sea. It was here that Mummy had once been crowned as a beauty queen. Its grand, but now grubby, concrete spaces still echo each summer with the shouts of bathers. Today it is packed with wet pink bodies as we hurry up to the changing rooms ranged along the top, and here my pudgy body is pushed and prodded into my new bikini and my hair pulled into pretty hair slides. Other small girls in their frocks and swimsuits stand holding their mothers' hands, waiting to approach a concrete pier that projects out into the huge round pool. The man in charge knows Mummy, as most people in Southport do. He gives her a big wink and we are moved up to the front of the queue.

Within moments I am being pushed out along this lonely catwalk. I stop, but Mummy tells me to go on.

'Don't be such a silly, just walk to the end and say hello to that nice man.'

She points to a figure at the far end of the pier. He beckons me to come and I totter bravely along, looking down at the water all around me. As I reach the end, he squats down beside me; his face is an odd colour, all puffy and tan foundation. He's smiling, has bright white teeth, and yet it's not like a proper smile. His face is now close to mine, and he says into a microphone that booms out from somewhere else, 'So! What is the name of this little Rosebud?'

I realize with horror that I am part of something I don't understand, and can't breathe.

He tries again, but not into the microphone and as if through his teeth. 'Just tell us your name, love?'

I finally manage to whisper: 'I'm Sally.'

I try to find my voice. He has pushed the microphone closer to me and I take a deep breath and shout. 'But I'm too shy!'

I hear my voice booming and bouncing back at me, mixed with a roaring laughter from all around the pool. The sound of it seems to hang in the air, and I turn and run back along the catwalk to my mother. I know that they are laughing at me because I have done it all wrong.

Mummy shakes her head, and points to the pink sashes on the table.

'Why did you run away? Look, they just wanted to give you a pretty Little Miss Rosebud sash, and put a crown on your head.'

I look over in wonder at the sashes, and then feel sadness that I have lost the crown and the chance to be something so special.

'You could have had the prize and the lovely sash to take home if you hadn't been such a sausage.'

We trudge home and I somehow already know that I am as disappointing as everything else in her grey world.

OUR HOUSE, 18 Saunders Street, was divided top and bottom and my nana lived upstairs and my parents and I downstairs. My father was already unwell with the sickness that would only get worse, but he still struggled out to his office most days. We had a gloomy living room with a brown sofa, rough to the touch, and a back door to a yard and small garden beyond. There was a fish-and-chip shop across the street where we got our dinner, groceries were delivered in a van, and a man called 'Joe the Hoover Man' came to mend things.

There were long summer days with drawn curtains when I was put in front of BBC children's shows that left me feeling upset and lonely. Torchy, the battery boy with his jerky movements, had strings you could see pulling on his puppet body. I remember hiding behind the sofa. I wanted something to wish for, but didn't know what it was.

Mum and me, 1960.

Even after my first failure there was still a grim determination hanging over my future. Aged three, I was enrolled at the Betty Bursey Dance Academy, and given a patent-leather case with a picture of ballet shoes on the front, to carry my shoes for ballet and tap. The older girls giggled in the changing room and whispered, 'Betty Bursey's busty', which she was. Afterwards Mummy and I practised song-and-dance routines at home in her bedroom, tapping to 'Bye, Bye Blackbird' and bending and tipping to 'I'm a Little Teapot'.

'Chin up and a pretty smile as you tip over, that's it. You are my special girl, you know?' she told me as she showed me the moves.

Once the memory of the Rosebud contest had faded a little, I was taken for a second try-out. It was another warm afternoon; we walked down to the seafront, on the promise of an ice cream, but then arrived at the large stage that was erected each season in the gardens outside the Floral Hall.

She bends and whispers, 'Go on, just sing "Wiggly Woo" like we do at home.'

I'm given a little shove, out in front of a sea of elderly day-trippers seated in deckchairs. A man holds the microphone for me to sing and off I go.

'There's a worm at the bottom of the garden, and his name is Wiggly Woo.'

I glance to the side of the stage, where Mummy is mouthing the words at me, and wiggling her hips and arms, to remind me to wiggle like a worm as I sing the chorus. But without her at my side I feel lost and alone; I falter and can't do my wiggle. As I curtsey, weak applause rises from the ranks of drowsy deckchairs.

With an air of finality my mother decided that I just could not sing, and that I had my father's 'two left feet' and would never dance. My role in the double act we were fated to be was yet to emerge. For the moment I was given up on until I could display a talent for something.

For now, we both knew who was the real star. There was a big gold chocolate box with a sagging bow of ribbon glued

to the top; it lived in wardrobes and I would beg for it to be lifted down and opened. Digging among the layers of photographs in different hues, I would pull them out longingly. These were small sepia windows to another life, and showed a little imp with dancing shoes and dressing up clothes grinning out at me.

WHO WAS SHE, this little girl? She was my mother, but in quite another incarnation, and living in this strange, dingy and unrecognizable world of the 'olden days'. If I caught her in the right mood, she could be drawn back there to the Liverpool dockyards, some twenty miles away from us in Southport. It was now only a few stops on the train, or a drive down past the sand dunes and through dull suburbs, past Auntie Grace's house, and past the war memorial and not so far at all; but it was also another place entirely: the past. Although it lay a little beyond my childish understanding, I would still feel the dark clouds of the Depression hanging heavily over Bootle's terraced slums, and the notorious Scotland Road roaring and rattling with life through those hard times. It was a place that was dirty, noisy and vivid. When the working day at the dockyards finished, the stream of men would head straight to the pubs, and by mid evening their doorways let out blasts of smoky air and maudlin drunken singing, until closing time when fights began on the pavements and the wives appeared, shouting, trying to get their husbands away home.

Nearby, at Uncle Charlie's coalyard, my mother – then Audrey Miller, aged six or seven – would be lifted onto the kitchen table, wearing her top hat, feet in shiny new tap shoes and clutching her cane. As the family crowded around she would start to sing, tapping her toes and swishing her cane from hand to hand, practising for her role in *Babes in the Wood*; the pantomime was to be performed at Liverpool's most splendid theatre, the Empire, and she was to be Bootle's very own leading light. Here she is with her shock of red hair, an irrepressible ball of impish energy, grabbing the limelight as she flutters by with the fairy chorus. 'Give us a turn!' someone calls. Immediately she stops dancing and pauses wide-eyed – she knows she has the room . . .

'Shhh and I'll tell you a secret,
something to open your eyes.
Are you awfully excited?
Cos it's going to be . . . a surprise!'

I learnt this same poem, widening my eyes, whispering the lines, just as she had done . . .

'Daddy says there aren't any fairies,
But Mummy whispers low.
"Don't take any notice, darling.
There are things even daddies don't know."'

This little girl would see things that I would never see, although I grew up with her, hearing her stories; and as I grew older I would begin to learn her secrets, and about the darker deeds she became caught up in. Something had happened in that shadowy world, something that would affect both our futures.

MOST DAYS Mummy and I strolled down to Lord Street, the graceful boulevard around which the town of Southport arranged itself. It stretched for almost a mile, wide enough to allow for expansive gardens, which ran continuously along its length. The elegant shop façades on the other side were fronted by a long cast-iron and glass canopy with fine detailing and ornate columns wrapped with plump cherubs. There were Tea Gardens, with playing fountains, and bandstands from which music was performed. Great chestnut trees made a cool canopy overhead.

In later years, when I lived in London, I would learn not to tell people that this was one of the finest thoroughfares in the world. It would make me seem ridiculous to be claiming this for a town no one knew and usually mixed up with Stockport. If I added that Prince Louis-Napoleon Bonaparte had lived here in 1846, and it had been the inspiration for Napoleon and Haussmann's scheme in redesigning Paris, I would be certainly mocked. But it was true, and in years to come, as I travelled the world, I would see great abandoned cities once on the Silk Route, or ruling a forgotten empire, and come to understand how easily one northern seaside town could be lost or buried under the silt of only a few decades of history.

My mother still had her postcards and pictures showing the town in the 1930s, when the rich and famous of the day came pouring out of the Garrick Theatre, the women in silks and furs, the men in evening wear and monocles. Uniformed chauffeurs waited in the glow of the street lamps, and behind them a thousand fairy lights glimmered in the trees.

Leading off from Lord Street were narrow lanes with small mysterious shops selling magical things. One grubby entrance was hidden beneath driftwood and dangling conch shells and guarded by a hanging African juju witch-doctor doll, and, even more terrifying, within, by a thin stooped old man. If you were brave enough to duck down and get past the fierce witch doctor, you came to broken steps leading to a basement cave where the old man's shell grotto sold everything it is possible to make from seashells. These barnacled wonders were some of the earliest things I can remember wanting.

Alongside him were second-hand booksellers mixed in with greasy cafés and tawdry bucket-and-spade shops with rows of bright pink sticks of rock. These lanes led from Lord Street's elegance to the part of town now judged to be 'common' and the Land of the Day-trippers. A grand Victorian promenade of large hotels, once the crown of the Riviera of the North West, was now beginning to tarnish, and beyond it the miles of pleasure gardens leading to the muddy beach were showing peeling paintwork and cracks thick with weeds.

Yet Lord Street still prospered, and incredibly an orchestra still played each day in the glass-domed restaurant of the Marshall and Snelgrove department store. This was where my mother longed to be, cocooned in its gilded calm, or at the Prince of Wales Hotel where people stepped out of

Rolls-Royces to vanish through great mahogany revolving doors into a world of luxurious wealth.

This world was now lost to her. All she had was me and my daddy, her terminally ill husband, and her life in a shabby flat. So she sighed and fidgeted through most of the day, played her gramophone records over and over again, smoking her menthol cigarettes.

She would sometimes leave me with Nana and disappear for hours, till my nana stood at the window with her Parkinson's tremor getting worse with the worry.

Sometimes mail arrived with foreign stamps, or someone telephoned from London, and my mother would brighten before falling into a deeper gloom.

My poor father, Neil, had reasons to believe that he had ruined the life of the woman he adored, and that his death would mean leaving me with a reluctant mother. Because of him, for some reason I would eventually come to understand, she hadn't been able to marry the man she really wanted to marry, or have the glittering life she had planned; and now he was going to leave her with no money.

Did he wonder how all this would play out when he was gone, and if she would begin to chase her lost dreams once again, but with me in tow, now fated to a rackety life? Did he fear what this would mean, and how it would shape my future?

He had contracted a rare disease while serving with the RAF in Africa during the war. He now struggled to carry on working, and increasingly he came home from the office to lie down or to go to his hospital visits.

None of this was the life that my mother had hoped for, and she was never a woman to simply accept her fate. One day we were going to be far away from it all. There was nothing else for it; she was so full of wanting, and still craving all the things that she believed had slipped away from her. To get these things back she was going to have to cross a line. I don't think she realized that this was what she was doing, or that she would be taking me with her to this life on the other side of that line; she was simply helpless and this was our fate. She had skills, honed in the back streets of Liverpool and learnt from her no-good father, which she was now quite willing to use to get her out of the mess in which she found herself, and who could blame her?

3

The Grand House

OUR TAXI PULLS UP at what seems to be a mansion. It is an enormous gloomy Victorian house of red brick smothered in a blanket of dense dusty ivy. Set back behind a busy main road, its gates open to a circular driveway and neat lawns with beds of black earth and rosebushes that point their spikes to the sky. Behind the front door is a vast tiled hallway, and then more corridors and doors. Just this hallway alone seems bigger than our entire previous flat. High ceilings look down onto rooms with new names: cloakroom, larder, dining room, salon . . . I have no memory of it having a kitchen at all and, if it did, I don't believe we ever used it.

A van arrives, and a small plump man who smells of perfume begins telling the other men where to put all the big boxes.

'Are you one of the Seven Dwarfs?'

Mummy says that was very rude and to say sorry. His name is David Glover, an antique dealer, and I watch as the stream of wooden crates begins to be unpacked; their contents are placed around the rooms and David Glover puts things on top of other things. A pillar called a torchère has a boy with wings and a bow and arrow placed on top of it; it means that you have to be very careful. In the dining room a great table of gleaming mahogany arrives, with an army of chairs to go around it that no one will ever sit on. The new furniture has names like Sheraton and Chippendale, and a sideboard called William the Third. I hide under this sideboard when Mummy's friends come round, and I hear the sparkly glasses taken out of the cabinet and the chink of a sherry bottle. I hear her friend, Auntie Ava, ask her 'How on earth have you afforded all this?' and my mother touches her nose and laughs, saying, 'That would be telling!'

Mum and Dad, (housekeeper in background)
14 Lulworth Road, 1962.

It is a house with a mystery: I find another den at the foot of the stairs from where I overhear my Auntie Grace whisper to Uncle Phil, 'How do you explain it, where's she finding all this money?'

It was clearly baffling to everyone that, just as we should have been sliding into poverty, we instead moved up in the world so spectacularly. My mother had no job, and her own mother, Nana, was mainly bedridden; my daddy was now very unwell, and there was me. Yet here we all were, and she had moved us from a shabby flat on the wrong side of town into a large and impressive house with live-in staff that she had apparently paid for herself. Even at a young age I was becoming aware of these secrets that seemed to hang in the air of those endless rooms.

FROM THE HALLWAY a sweeping staircase wound up to a landing and corridor, off which there were numerous bedrooms. At night the stairwell felt even bigger, leading to a pool of darkness below. It was a house that changed shape under cover of night. Corridors stretched out forever, the stairs doubled their length and there were strange noises, whisperings and banged doors.

At the top of the staircase there was a door. This door was quite unlike all the others in the house. The others were of dark wood with brass, but this was painted white and had a plastic handle. This door led to another world, one so different it was hard to believe the two regions shared a roof. Through this door was the domain of 'the Back Flat'. Here a succession of housekeepers lived a completely self-contained existence: in a warm, cheery fug, with a smell of sausages, and windows that streamed with condensation from the gas fire.

The Back Flat had colourful lino and carpets, and a display of decorative objects that changed with each house-keeper but somehow shared a cheeky style, and seemed of a quite different order than the objects that had been carefully positioned around the main house.

Some of these ladies came with husbands and some without. First was Alice, Irish, with pale powdery skin she liked me to kiss; then Mrs Liddel with her colostomy bag that smelt bad; then Mr and Mrs Braithwaite with their son Colin who wasn't quite right; and there were others long since forgotten. They all lived similar domestic lives, in the glare of bright overhead fluorescent lighting, with TVs on loudly in the kitchen showing *Opportunity Knocks* or *Coronation Street*.

The housekeepers had stacks of family photographs of smiling grandchildren and mementoes from holidays, things that made me long to go on a holiday: straw donkeys in hats, a mermaid made of seashells, tea towels emblazoned with lines like 'Glorious Devon'. From her beloved Ireland Alice brought hundreds of knick-knacks in vivid green, with wink-ing leprechauns and shamrocks that brought you good luck.

Mrs Liddel's 'piggywigs' peeped out from the window ledges, alongside decorated mugs and tea cosies; Mrs Braith-waite had her 'plaques', plaster sculptures which crowded the walls from their hooks – pirate ships, glades with Gypsy caravans, lagoons with Venetian gondolas and the heads of flamenco dancers. She gave me one for my room, of a pirate buccaneer with a beard who leered down at me, and I loved it passionately.

They all were happy to feed me my preferred dinner of a chip butty and a cup of sweet tea before sending me back through the door to the gloomy spaces of the landing. I hated going back across that threshold.

The Back Flat was slightly awkward and not where I belonged, but it was cosy. The Other Side, our house and my bedroom, felt dark and cold after my mother had gone out, and I was ashamed that I had to have a potty under the bed as I was too frightened to put my head outside the covers, let alone cross the landing and go down the long creaking corridor to the toilet.

As an only child adrift in this great pile of a house, I loved to hear stories of my mother's Bootle sardine-can childhood. If on a rainy day I could coax her to bring down that box, I would rummage through the treasure trove of photographs, pulling out this one or that, pleading with her to fill in the soundtrack, to conjure the atmosphere to go with these fading images. Life at Uncle Charlie's sounded so safe, cocooned against the poverty and violence outside.

There everyone was bundled in together around the warm fire, with the sound and smell of the horses steaming and stamping in the yard outside. Charlie Clarke's own large family ruled the roost. 'Nana and I just mucked in, sleeping together in a small bed and sharing a room with the cousins.'

'Was it really, really cosy?' I'd ask hopefully.

'Yes I suppose it was, but very cramped and noisy. From dawn to dusk you could hear wagons clattering about in the coalyard and horses clopping in and out, and people shouting and joshing. There was always a great pot of Scouse on the stove, and it seemed to go with the endless chatter around the table: the *craic*.'

My mother soaked it up, as I would soak up her tales in turn: the gossip, banter and stories of her Irish family roots, friends and neighbours, in which everyone was either a saint or a sinner. Words and thoughts came tumbling out of her, her cousins would later tell me, as she was lifted onto that table to entertain, to relate the story of some small triumph or disaster to make everyone laugh or cry. She made the stories crackle with life; she could just get people, their voices and little tics. It was a gift and she was going to make it work for her. She was going to be somebody; her mother Rebecca knew it, and was quietly determined. Audrey had absorbed this into her being, understanding that she was special, and one day her life would be somewhere else far from those dirty streets.

This was where our history started; I never heard any of the Irish past from further back, except that I was told that my grandparents – Rebecca, my nana, and Len, my grandfather – had arrived here from Ireland just before Audrey, my mother, was born. She would describe the dockyard slums, built around *courts*, dirt-floored yards where there was a toilet and a tap shared by several families.

'Nana was a real lady, and an angel,' my mother always said, but I knew she had married a bad man, my grandfather,

Mum, Bootle, 1932.

Len Miller. The family story was that he was a man with some plausible charm, which soon wore thin, revealing him as a charlatan and an operator. Nana quietly managed to get by, keeping house and her pride and doting on her small daughter.

Then Len disappeared, leaving them destitute. Without his income they were homeless and had to move in down the road with Uncle Charlie. Nana took on a coster barrow to sell fruit and vegetables. We had driven past that bleak stretch of road down by the docks, and my mother had pointed out to me where Nana had stood with her barrow all day and in all weathers.

'But every night Nana twisted the rags round my hair with her poor sore fingers that were chapped from the cold, and in the morning, when they were unwound, my ringlets would tumble down past my shoulders. People would stop me in the street to exclaim at my hair.'

'What did they say?' I asked, wishing my own brown mop was long glossy red-gold ringlets.

'They'd say, "Look at that colour, true auburn, and the shine to it. The glory of it," they'd say.'

'Tell me again about the parades?' These were the kinds of questions she liked me to ask her: invitations to tell a story from those years when they were still happy and full of hope.

'In the spring I'd be put in a dress made from lace table-cloths with a crown of flowers, and I'd ride just like a princess on top of Uncle Charlie's coal wagon at the head of the May Day Parade.'

'And where would you go?' I'd ask, staring at the little black and white picture of the small Queen who stared back at me. She was my age, grinning at me, but from this other sooty and shadowy world.

'We'd trundle down through the park, where I'd sit grandly on a special throne, with crowds all around watching me being crowned as Queen of May.'

'Did they all cheer?'

'I expect they did. Then in the summer it was the Orange Day Parade and I would be the Good King Billy, wearing a big floppy hat with an enormous feather. Uncle Charlie's horse carried me all round the streets of Bootle.'

I loved this bit, and would ask: 'And what was it that they shouted at you?'

'The Protestants all cheered us, but the Catholics yelled at us, like they did in the playground, "Proddy dogs!" And me and my friends shouted back, "Cat licks!"'

I'd peer at the photos of Mummy in her finery and imagine being there, and yelling 'Cat licks!' too.

Her happiest moments of all were on stage, in her fairy wings and ballet dress made by Auntie Sadie, her godmother and her mother's younger best friend. The two women were very different. Rebecca, my nana, was quiet and modest, whereas Sadie had the same high spirits as Audrey.

'People would think I was Sadie's little girl, as the two of us would be laughing and skipping along the road while my mother walked quietly behind us. "No, I'd say, she's my fairy godmother!"'

Sadie was a waitress in a big department store. The wealthy merchant patrons were often generous with their tips, and she liked to spoil her little god-daughter. One day Sadie treated Rebecca and Audrey to an outing in the nearby resort of Southport. Despite being just a few miles from Liverpool, Audrey felt they had travelled far away from the grimy streets of Bootle. 'I had a postcard which I pinned by my bed with its view of that magical place and on it was printed SOUTHPORT, RIVIERA OF THE NORTH WEST. Riviera! I dreamt of a life there, sitting sipping tea beneath those trees around the bandstand, an orchestra playing, then in the evening stepping out of a shiny car to disappear into one of the grand hotels.'

It was only as I got older that she told me how much their lives had changed when, one cold winter night, a cousin had burst into the kitchen at Uncle Charlie's. Had they heard the news? 'Len Miller's been seen back in Liverpool, and he's looking for Rebecca and the girl.'

'I was thrilled at first. I'd been so small when my father left and I'd invented a whole life for him, telling the other children about his heroic deeds in some distant country. I think I started to think it was all real. So, when I first saw him standing there, I couldn't believe that this hunched, weasly little man, smelling of drink, was really my own daddy.'

Worse still, he'd come to claim her. Her life would not be the same again, and I was already living with many of the consequences.

It was hard for me to imagine a daddy who was horrible. One door from the first-floor landing of our house was often closed, and this was the room where my own father lay very ill; the days when he felt better were fewer and fewer.

When we first moved to this house we would both go down to the workshop he had set up in the cellar, and I longed for him to get well enough to do this again. The workshop had a delicious smell of wood and glue, and here he would build miraculous things such as record players and cocktail cabinets. He would lift me onto the workbench and let me 'help'. I'd hold the frame down as he carefully glued onto it the wooden bas-relief shape of a puppy that he had carved specially for me. Leading from the carpentry workshop was a darkroom, pitch-black except for a red glow, and here we would develop the pictures he had taken. If the chemical smell was too strong I'd bury my head in his jumper, and he'd hug me so I could breathe in his lovely clean soapy smell. He worked quietly and intently, but every now and then he would peer at me through the darkness and say, 'Where is she, where's my little helper?'

'Here I am!' I could just make him out in the gloom. He'd lift the negatives up, choosing which to print – me, smiling just for him, freckled and happy. He would squint at each one and say, 'Yes, here she is! And here she is again, even prettier! How ever will we choose?'

These images, and the cine films he made, became an alternative version of my childhood and fixed forever my memories of him. They would capture these years in such shimmering colour and light that they seemed to obliterate the reality of it altogether.

Gradually these days of making things from wood, or being absorbed in his darkroom with its clicking enlargers and splicing tables, became less frequent; his days of playing with me were also coming to an end, his energy draining from him till he became silent and solitary in his room. I would be told to let him rest. I would sit outside his door on the floor, with my book, feeling in some way that I was guarding him against danger, although I understood that really the danger was inside him. Sometimes I was allowed to go in and lie quietly on his bed. If he was asleep I would lie very still and watch him breathing, looking not ill but just tired.

Me, 1961.

The landing felt like a scary place, as across from Daddy's door was Nana's room, and from behind it came sounds of moaning and yelling. Nana was always either in bed or in her deep armchair, shaking and confused from her worsening Parkinson's. Often I was sent in by my mother to clear the ghost people that were upsetting her. Nana would wave and shout at these people that I couldn't see, but after I'd shooed them out and told her that they were now 'all gone' she would lie back with a sigh of relief. It was my special job and I did it as thoroughly as I could. But she'd then doze off and wake to find the 'people' had come back to torment her, and so the cycle would begin again. It was a house of sickness, and no wonder my mother wanted to get away from it whenever she could.

4

The Riviera of the North West

THE BEST PART OF THE DAY was spent sitting in the gorgeousness of Marshall and Snelgrove's restaurant with my mother, eating a banana split while the orchestra played, the violin mingling with the soft buzz of adult chatter. Elegant model girls in their gowns approached each table, delicately holding placards with the price, always in guineas, and they would do a pretty twirl to show off the dress to all its advantage.

Auntie Ava would often be with us, and she and Mummy would talk to them about the 'cut' of the gown and discuss the style and colour. I loved the words they used. 'Would you say that was fuchsia or mauve?' 'The silk mohair has a lovely sheen, and don't you love the dear little sweetheart neckline?' The model smilingly chatted with them, as they fingered the delicious fabrics.

I'm not sure when it was that I first heard one or two of these young women described as Mummy's 'girls'. Was it overheard, or was it ever whispered to me gently, some kindly hand on my arm somewhere out of the softness, across the plush dreaminess of the afternoon?

What did it mean, that in some curious way these beautiful creatures, along with a girl who worked in the make-up department, were connected with my mother? This fed the slight unreality that I sometimes sensed my mother floated in, and me with her; but in the respectable elegance of Marshall's restaurant the willowy young women simply appeared to be queenly creatures.

But then I would slip off away from them to explore, and feel that exhilarating thrill of freedom and excitement with the huge department store as my territory.

I'd begun to have dreams, that would recur for the rest of my life, of discovering a door in a house that I've lived in for some time, a house that has become my home, and yet there is a door I've never noticed before, until quite suddenly it opens into a new world that is all mine: it may be a glittering ballroom with great doors onto a maze of walled gardens with fountains where people greet me as if they know me, or a palm house with an intricate webbing of glass and cast-iron tracery soaring above me with all kinds of strange plants thronged with colourful birds and people gathered in its secret corners. My excitement was always intense at these discoveries and it began then, during my forays into these old shops and hotels off Lord Street, as if from them there arose ghosts from a different age.

I began to see that the immediate world beyond that unhappy house, Southport itself, was full of promise. What had been such a wonderland for Audrey, as a child, became one for me now, and Marshall and Snelgrove department store and the Prince of Wales Hotel were its great pleasure palaces, full of endless possibilities for exploring. In my own head this was who I was: 'an explorer'.

Some of my forays and adventures would take place while my mother was with Auntie Ava, her only friend. Ava was, by common agreement, the most beautiful woman in Southport. She looked and dressed like a nineteen forties movie star, and still wore in the more casual decade of the 1960s what my mother called 'picture hats', with a wide brim to frame her chocolate eyes and moon-pale skin. She spent a lot of time in bed, and was seen by people as a little 'odd'. She could be funny, and even astute, but she had an air of childlike naivety and seemed to be incapable of doing the simplest of things. It was therefore hard to judge whether she was unaware of, or chose to ignore, my mother's unusual lifestyle.

Ava's husband, Anthony, with his cravats and immaculate blazers had the suave looks of a matinee idol. He didn't go to work and loathed my mother, for taking Ava away from him for so much of the day. He also feared that Ava's friendship could affect their own reputation, which he cared about enormously.

Anthony and Ava sat every summer's day on a kind of stage set outside their house. They'd had the brick wall in their front garden specially lowered so that the whole town could see them there, on their elaborate patio adorned with beautiful furniture and parasols, dressed as if for Ascot, but simply taking afternoon tea brought out by the housekeeper. Buses went past and people pointed; they were famous locally for their gracious, old-fashioned appearance and general eccentricity.

Perhaps it was Ava's oddness that inured her, or maybe attracted her, as a fellow outsider, to my mother's outcast status. For Audrey was increasingly ostracized by the town and this exclusion soon extended to Ava for being my mother's close friend.

During the times when my mother was in Southport their routine was always the same. Ava would spend the morning getting ready for Audrey to collect her at eleven for morning coffee at Marshall's. After my own treat of an ice cream or teacake, I would be sent off to play. I had several favourite routines. One was to visit the make-up counters where the attractive ladies would let me try on perfume and put lipstick on me. Another trick was to goad the lift man; he seemed to dislike children, and would be mean and pompous if I rode up and down between floors with no purpose. My favourite pastime of all was to visit the manager.

This involved getting past his fierce secretary who sat behind a desk outside his office clacking away at a big black typewriter which pinged occasionally. I would stand politely before her, asking 'Could I please, please say hello to the manager?' Sometimes she would just say no, and that he was very busy, but sometimes she would say that she would ask him, although she expected he *was* very busy. Usually the answer came back that I could go in, but just for two minutes, as he was really very busy. The manager, Mr Naylor, sat in a wood-panelled office behind a large desk. The routine was always the same.

'And what can I do for you today, young lady?' he would ask.

'Please can you make a swan for me?' I would beg.

He would then take a packet of cigarettes from his drawer, pull out the silver paper, and twist it into a delicate swan shape which he would present to me with a flourish. The charm lay in my knowing that this busy man had set aside a few minutes of his day for me, and also in the lovely masculine smell of tobacco that filled his office and could be revisited later by sniffing my swan.

When she was not with Ava my mother was always out. The housekeepers in the Back Flat were more and more responsible for my welfare and the house the other side of the door became quieter and quieter.

My mother was not at home most nights, but where does she go? There are whispers and murmurs that have now become familiar to me, like a soft insistent mantra. 'There's a new crowd arrived at the Prince' is one. Another is 'Peter Cooper is in town', which always gives me a thrill in the pit of my stomach.

Peter Cooper sweeps into our hallway like a tornado, his black eyes shining from under a big Russian hat.

He shouts, 'My little Aud,' and sweeps my mother up in his arms and whirls her round and round.

I shout, 'My turn!' and he does the same for me, spinning me till I'm dizzy.

'You look like a Russian Cossack in that hat, a wicked

Peter Cooper in a Russian hat.

marauding Cossack,' she tells him, and he does a Russian dance right there in our hallway, his arms folded and his legs flying out.

'Then bring your Cossack his vodka and caviar,' he roars.

She gets him a drink and tells him that she's missed him, and that she can feel herself coming back to life. Then she says 'OK! It's Showtime!' Which is something she says when fun things are about to happen.

I know that she will now be busy arranging parties and dates for him and his friends and, if I'm lucky, I'll go with her and be able to watch all the excitement.

Peter Cooper is the King of Southport. He grew up,

like my mother, around the Liverpool dockyards, and had invented a way of welding ships underwater and made an instant fortune. He now lives on a Californian beach with his millions and a beautiful wife, but can never bear to be away from his mates or his home town for long. It is always one big party from the day he arrives in town until the day he leaves and my mum's job is to make that party happen. To me he fills the sky. Huge, restless, raven haired, with his booming voice and wicked laugh he is the pirate-buccaneer plaque on my bedroom wall come to life. Sitting on a bar stool, in a charming mood I can imagine him as James Bond twirling his cocktail stick, and now I can add 'wild Cossack' to my Peter Cooper fantasy list.

My father is upstairs, very sick, and I hear half-whispered conversations between him and my mum. His voice is so weak now. She sounds kind and gentle, but firm.

She is telling him she is going out. He doesn't ask where, or who with.

'When do you think you'll be back?'

'Not too late,' she promises, but it isn't true. She will be late.

'I'll see you in the morning. You sleep now' – and she kisses him.

'Tell Sally to come in.'

I've been waiting for this, listening at the door. She comes out and says that I can go in and sit with him.

'Quietly, mind. Don't tire him out with too much chatter.' So I sit on the edge of the bed, and try to talk in a soft voice and tell him about things that are cheerful.

I show him the things I've made for him: drawings, or stories and poems I've written, as he likes that. After a while, his head falls back onto the pillow and he looks exhausted.

'Shall I tuck you in?' I love to kiss him, and do this as if he was the child. Sometimes when I leave him I want to cry, but I don't let him see this. When I'm called away, I go through to the Back Flat for my tea, and wait for the housekeeper to tell me when to go to bed.

During the day I can sometimes go out with my mother and if Peter Cooper is in town, or there is an important crowd at the Prince, we go there. Aside from those two palaces to our kingdom, Marshall and Snelgrove department store, and 'the Prince', there was a third, the Kingsway Casino. But 'the Kingsway' was barred to children, which only made it more tantalizing as I peered in past the bouncers to the huge chandeliers and forbidden sumptuous spaces beyond. Inside I would see my mother deep in conversation with someone, doing 'business' as she called it, and I knew I had to wait patiently or next time I might be left at home.

'The Prince' was a grand hotel that seemed to me like the centre of the world. Through the great doors with their uniformed footmen was a blazing coal fire and, at Christmas, a swan carved of ice. Ava and Anthony stayed there every year when their housekeeper was on holiday, and Audrey and I would visit for lavish teas. And the rest of the year my mother was a constant visitor to the lounge and bar areas where she was often 'talking business'.

If she had to take me with her, I would be told to go and 'explore'.

'Scoot and skidaddle, go away and have fun,' she'd say, sending me off with a blown kiss, and I would run away to lose myself for hours. Through one set of double doors off the thickly carpeted corridors was a grand ballroom with a glass dome and a sweeping staircase leading up to a balcony. My mother had showed me this room and told me about her New Year's Eve surprise:

'They wheeled me in right here to the middle of the ballroom dance floor. I was crouching down in the trolley with a tablecloth over it, so they couldn't see me. There was a huge iced cake on top that I could stand up in.'

She demonstrated, crouching down. 'Then they started the countdown: ten – *doing*! Nine – *doing*! Eight – *doing*!'

I joined in with her. On the last chime she leapt up, showing me how on the final chime of midnight, she would burst forth in a sequined costume.

'Happy New Year!'

'And were all the people at the party terribly amazed?'

'Astonished! They couldn't see that the cake had a crêpe-paper top. And then I would throw streamers and the band would play.'

Alone in the ballroom's splendour I would reenact this moment of breaking through the crêpe-paper ceiling, covered in glitter, my arms aloft, to loud applause, as the orchestra struck up 'Auld Lang Syne' and I threw streamers towards the cheering crowd.

My other playground was the ladies' cloakroom, with dressing tables and tall mirrors with hinged flaps that you could stand in the middle of. If you wrapped the mirrored flaps around yourself, you would see hundreds of little girls just like me trapped in glass rooms. I would wave to them and longed to reach them, but they only waved back.

By early evening the Rolls-Royces and Jags would be three deep in the car park and the Prince bar would be in full swing, alive with laughter and gossip. I longed to go into that rich fug of brandy fumes, expensive scent and smoke. Mink coats, silky, gleaming and cool to the touch, were flung carelessly across the sofas under the jealous stares of women who had yet to be given one. My own mother's mink was one of the loveliest, with a dark soft glow to the fur a high collar around her long neck and buttons studded with diamonds.

'Just feel that,' she would say dreamily, in a moment of rare satisfaction, shaking her head at the deliciousness of it.

There were brief moments, longed for, and longingly remembered, when the town drew the world to it, and these moments saved my mother's life. Royal Birkdale Golf Club was nearby, and brought big international players, wealthy golfers, dukes and earls, to town for the weeks of the tournament. The Prince Hotel would host lavish dinners in the ballroom, and even the prime minister, Harold Wilson, came to watch the golf. My mother had some dealings with all this that were secret, and that I didn't understand, but they added to the excited buzz of the place in an indefinable way.

The less glamorous side to our life was 'the shops' – my mother's shops. I wasn't sure how many there were, or what went on in them. I think they all looked the same: seedy rooms on back streets with blacked-out windows covered with a mesh grille. I would usually be told to wait in the car, but sometimes I would go in and sit on a stool while she talked to whoever worked there. There was a Formica counter where an old man sat smoking, and the walls were usually covered with the pinned-up racing pages of the newspaper. One shop had a row of horseshoes over the door, and my mother explained, 'See, they must always be that way up, like a U, to hold all our luck inside and not let any of it out.'

But I imagined all our luck in there, and worried that someone might one day turn them upside down. The shops were never full – usually there were just one or two other men, shuffling about – and if a race was on there was a speaker that droned out the crackling commentary . . .

It was a strangely soporific chant, like drowsy wasps buzzing, trapped against the window on a hot day. It was supposed to be exciting, but instead it seemed to me like the most dull sound in the world, the essence of boredom.

It was only as I became a little older that I realized that the shops were in some way connected with things that had happened in my mother's childhood. Little by little it came out, as I asked my innocent questions and gazed at those old photographs. What was so bad about the small squinting man beside her and her mother? If that was really her daddy, why did she hate him so much?

5

Bookie's Runner

IN A CERTAIN MOOD, my mother would forget that I was a child and, spellbound by her own story, she would let slip the secrets of her early life. Forgetting her audience, she would begin to relive it and I would see it all come back, flickering in her eyes: the dirty windowpanes, light slicing through the smoke from the fire, and her father edgy, his muscles twitching like a hair trigger.

'The girl has to go into the pubs; the other children do it, the job needs it, the money's got to be made.' They were both devastated by what he was suggesting Audrey now had to do.

I didn't understand why my mother might sometimes tell people about this time of her life as if it was another amusing anecdote about her rackety past. 'Of course, I was a bookie's runner, as a child. While you were playing nicely in the park, I was going round the pubs taking bets and dodging the police.'

It wouldn't be told to a lady, but to someone like Peter Cooper or one of his crowd; then she could make it sound like a rather racy thing to have done, although I knew that it had sickened her. Her father was something called a 'turf accountant'. This was his new 'business', an illegal enterprise which he announced to the family on his return, and my mother, aged only nine or ten, was to work for him.

'He could see I was perfect for the job, and if the police came into the pubs and asked what I was doing I'd to say my ma had sent me to fetch my father.'

'Could he have gone to prison?' I'd ask, urging her to give me as many gory details as possible.

'Yes, the police were always after us. We'd come running back from the pubs with all the bets, and hide under this big tarpaulin he had in the back yard. We had to put them in the "clock bag", a leather bag that had a clock set to the time, so when the bag was sealed it showed the bets had been put in before the race started. Sometimes the other bookies, the McGanns, would come after us or tip off the police, and there would be a terrific kerfuffle.'

At night the pubs were warm and steamy, the floors sticky underfoot with spilt beer and a crunch of sawdust and cigarette butts. The public bar heaved with men – all men, except for her, the one small girl, weaving her way through it all, taking the punts. Sometimes a gentlemanly arm would help her, parting the throng of leery bodies, propping each other up, so she could pass. Mouths opened near her face, a gaping pink wetness with missing teeth, rasping their demands for this bet or that. So it went on until at last she would be pushing through those swing doors and out onto the street. It would take a moment to collect herself, and then she would run.

She shuddered. 'They would be drunk, and saying terrible, disgusting things to me, and touching me.' She hinted at something worse.

I believed that the rest of the story had something to do with the little coat. In the top of my mother's wardrobe, next to the box of photographs, were a few tantalizing treasures, and among them was a tiny, precious coat with a fur collar. It was wrapped in tissue paper and kept beside my mother's first pink satin ballet shoes. I longed to know about this carefully preserved memento, but, just like her account of what took place around the pubs, she would always stop before the end. It was only ever a tale half told.

The worst part of her life in the pubs had been returning with the betting results and dealing with men who may have lost all the money they had. Their drunken self-pity would turn to anger and the bookie's daughter was an easy target. 'I couldn't tell my mother what some of them did to me. It would have hurt her so much to know what went on.'

'What went on? And what happened to Sadie doll?'

My mother had told me about the doll with the china face and eyes that opened and shut. She'd come on a boat all the way from America, and no one in the street or the whole of Bootle had seen anything like her, or the clothes that Sadie doll had, her little coat with frog buttons and fur cuffs. But when I asked where she was now, my mother would say, 'Oh, she got broken.'

Slowly, over the years, the story would be told, of how her mother, Rebecca, had pleaded with Len not to send Audrey

Rebecca Miller, 'Nana'.

into the pubs again, but then she would say the wrong thing and he'd lash out, pulling out his thick leather belt.

Loop by loop, burnt into Audrey's memory, that belt and the slow intention of it. The air filling with horror and Audrey escaping, hiding in the bedroom, but she could still hear that awful sound; it went on and on . . . and then there was silence.

It was only when I was older that I heard how the Sadie doll lay on the floor after one of these violent outbursts from her father, the doll's pretty pink cheek smashed, and Audrey couldn't look at it. Her mother had to hide the doll and the coat so that Audrey would stop crying.

Audrey tried to tell her father that she couldn't do the job any more, and the abuse he had turned on her mother now rained down on her. She saw her mother change during these years, and begin to lose hope. The little doll's coat was always kept, as a memory of their past life. There were no more dancing classes or days out now; life became a grim round of humiliation and fear.

Then war broke out and saved her. In 1939, Liverpool's dockyards were a prime target for the German bombers and soon they came. Rebecca and Sadie felt that evacuation could only be better for Audrey than the life she would be leaving behind, and so, aged thirteen, she joined the thousands of Merseyside children taken to Lime Street station to escape the bombing.

'What was it like, being sent away?' I peered at the gloomy house and imagined the small girl in the pictures being sent off on a train, a label pinned to her coat, leaving her mother to live with complete strangers.

'As the train crowded with children pulled out of Lime Street station, some of the little ones were screaming for their mothers. I saw one mother being sick on the platform, but mine managed to stand tall as she waved me off. I was already missing her, and terrified that we didn't know where we were going. I'd never been away from her before. Then, once we were out of Liverpool, I started to recognize the names of the stations – Freshfield, Formby . . . – and I knew that we must be headed for Southport I felt much better then.

'When we arrived we all walked in a long crocodile to the Southport Evacuee Centre. There was a hall where a lady made all of us children line up till a nurse came and tugged a comb through our hair. It was full of disinfectant, which smelt horrible. We waited for ages, until someone came and took me over to meet this smartly dressed man. He was introduced to us as Mr Grimshaw, and he took me and two other girls and drove us away in a big comfortable car, all sitting on the leather back seat. Mr Grimshaw asked us all sorts of questions about our families and homes. The other two girls didn't say much, so I did my best, answering politely, and thought that I'd made a good impression. Soon we turned into a wide leafy street with large houses surrounded by gardens.'

There was a house we sometimes drove past, and which my mother would point out to me. 'There it is, that big house there behind the hedges.'

I'd peer at the plain red-brick villa and try to imagine arriving there to live with strangers.

'Did it seem enormous?' I'd ask.

'Yes, it seemed like a palace; it had a large front door and the entrance hall opened out to a grand staircase. It was so warm, with soft thick carpets which seemed to muffle the sound so everything felt cocooned.'

'And what happened then?'

'From a slightly open door off the hall, I could hear the sounds of the radio, and from there Mrs Grimshaw came out to greet us. Through the door we could see right into the sitting room and there a boy and girl, only a little younger than me, were playing a game around the sofa. There was a delicious smell of cooking from the kitchen. It was the kind of family that I had always dreamt of belonging to, and now here it was and I was going to become a part of it.'

'And then what?' I knew, but I wanted to hear it all again.

'The three of us were shown up to a cold attic room, and at dinnertime our meal was brought up to us on a tray by a housekeeper. Mrs Grimshaw came up to say goodnight. Downstairs we knew that the family were all eating together and I was just looking forward to the next day and meeting them properly.'

It was only after a few days that Audrey realized this was how things would always be. She had still barely spoken to the Grimshaw children, and it was the housekeeper who dealt with the evacuees. Now when I looked out of the car window at the house it appeared like a prison as I imagined the lonely girl in the attic, hearing the sounds of family life going on downstairs but never allowed to join in.

It wasn't long before her mother and Sadie visited from Liverpool to take her out for the day. They were sorry to hear how the Grimshaws were treating her, but she realized that they weren't surprised. After the Princess fantasy that they had spun around her she had believed she was special, and it was only now that she understood how people like this – with their big house and grand furniture – might actually see a girl like her: she was a slum child, suspected of having bad ways as well as lice or diseases. The Grimshaws sent her to a different school from their own children, and kept her away from them at home in case of contamination. And Audrey woke up to the fact that this was what her future looked like, and she would eventually be returning to that world.

She only coped with that isolation in the Grimshaws' attic by planning her brilliant escape when she had got away from her father and built a new life.

The sequence of photographs in my mother's chocolate box, which provided such vivid glimpses of her childhood, had nothing to offer for those bleak early-evacuee years of the war. There was no doting mother and godmother to record her changing during this time from the impish child to a young woman. Those two years were strangely blank. The only thing she told me was that her first period had been upsetting and humiliating, as Mrs Grimshaw handed her sanitary towels to use, without telling her what to do with them afterwards. She had tried to smuggle them out of the house to find somewhere to get rid of them, a situation that left her dreading every month that followed.

As Audrey turned fifteen she finally saw her first chance and grabbed onto it. 'I met Jean at a Saturday dancing class and noticed her straight away. She had these wide blue eyes and soft blonde hair, and she appeared to float as she danced. It was almost as if she knew that her life was going to be easy and happy, and she could just drift into that wonderful future that was waiting for her.'

I knew Mummy's friend, who became my Auntie Jean, was pretty and clever; she later travelled the world playing international bridge tournaments, and the friendship had lasted years with Christmas cards always exchanged. Back then Jean had loved Audrey's reckless spirit and energy, and

Audrey was fascinated by Jean's gentle manners. A boy at school had called Audrey 'a bog-Irish minx' and now, when she looked in the mirror at her dark red hair and her lively, shrewd face, she doubted for the first time that she was really as beautiful as Sadie and her mother had told her she was.

She found herself envying Jean's soft angelic features as much as the lavish bedroom, with its swagged curtains, in the big villa. Jean's parents were as kind as she was, and made Audrey feel welcome. Later she told me that this had opened her eyes to something she thought was really important: that it was much easier to be good and kind if you had everything, and she advised me to 'make friends with girls who are rich and beautiful, as they won't be jealous or mean. They can afford to be nice.'

This was simply a pragmatic idea, not something fed by envy and self-doubt, which weren't generally part of her nature. There was a natural confidence that would bubble back up in her as soon as life offered her a break. If any door opened an inch she would immediately push it as hard as she could, and once open she would dash through it, certain of something marvellous on the other side. Now a door opened, as she told Jean's parents about the Grimshaw's unfriendliness and the illegal work that her father had forced her into and they offered to help. They took Audrey in to live with them until she was on her feet, and Jean's father, who worked in newspapers, found her a job helping on the local paper, the *Southport Visitor*. She was taken on to answer the phone and make tea, but stayed after work each night, teaching herself to type.

Mum, dressed for success.

'I'd seen the Hollywood film *His Girl Friday*, with Rosalind Russell as the glamorous newspaper reporter. So I pinned up a picture of her sitting at her typewriter, wearing a sexy pinstripe suit, to inspire me to work harder.' 'Always dress for the role you aspire to, remember that!' was one of her tips.

She had also read about the Hollywood gossip columns of Hedda Hopper, a society journalist famous for her extraordinary hats. She would sometimes balance silly things on her head to make me laugh – a colander with a saucepan on top, or my teddy – and sing a song, 'A Hat for Hedda Hopper', and do a comical dance.

My mother went to the cinema once or twice a week if she could, and not only did she know every star, but their private lives and paths to success that she had pored over in her favourite *Picturegoer* magazine. It depicted the unimaginably glamorous lives of the actors who had left Britain for Hollywood, such as Vivien Leigh, who had scooped the lead role of the century as the Irish American Southern belle Scarlett O'Hara in *Gone with the Wind*.

The Civil War epic was the biggest film of that era, and Scarlett was my mother's heroine, who brushed aside any setbacks with a 'fiddle-de-dee'. The image of Scarlett kneeling amongst the war-ravaged ruins of her plantation home, holding up a handful of soil and passionately declaring, 'As God is my witness, I'll never go hungry again,' became Audrey's talisman: a girl who did whatever she had to do to get what she needed.

At sixteen Audrey now believed she might escape the Liverpool slums for ever and find a way of bringing her mother to the safety of Southport. She longed to be a part of Jean's social set, but knew she was still an outsider from a different class. She might copy their voices and manners, but it was not enough. Jean and her friends had all been to the same private school, and went together to smart dances and parties to which Audrey wasn't invited. The new job then gave her an idea. Inspired by gossip columnist Hedda Hopper and the magazines she loved, she worked hard to learn how to write in their style. Her schooling had been poor, and writing didn't come easily to her, until she learnt to say something out loud and then get it down. She also studied the language of the gossip magazines and copied their sentence structure and at last was able to offer the editor of the *Southport Visitor* his own social column. She handed him her sample draft, called 'Talk of Many Things with Audrey Miller', which she had decorated with little drawings copied from magazine adverts of champagne bottles and bubbles, and high-heeled shoes.

Now she had an open invitation to the elegant dances at Royal Birkdale Golf Club that Jean and her friends went to. She borrowed Jean's pretty and more ladylike clothes, and was now given a warm welcome at 21st-birthday parties, where she would describe their 'charming home and wonderful hospitality'. There was always an added smattering of gossip: 'Those-in-the-know are whispering about a wedding between a certain Miss Bailey and a Mr Howard; there was definitely romance in the air on this occasion. Those watching the dancing were heard to comment, "Oh yes, it's love all right!"'

Other weeks the local news was clearly thin on the ground: 'Have you heard? Party girl Ida Hughes may be settling down at last, having purchased a sewing machine – "Hey, need anything special running up, girls?"'

This was how she could become the girl that her mother and godmother had dreamt she would be. Suddenly she had invitations to every event in town and, with some cast-off evening dresses of Jean's and notebook in hand she could go anywhere.

6

Goodbyes

AUNTIE GRACE was standing in the hallway with a hankie, trying not to cry. She and Uncle Phil had come to take me to the cinema to see *Flipper*, a film about a dolphin, as my birthday treat. I'd been to the Marshall and Snelgrove salon to have a birthday hairdo, a shampoo and set, and had spent the morning happily side by side with my mother under the hairdryers, reading the grown-up magazines. This was supposed to be a special evening, but it now felt at risk of being spoilt.

Grace had just been in to see my father, and was coming out of his room when my mother appeared from her adjoining bedroom.

'What on earth?' Grace said sharply. She looked my mother up and down in disgust.

Audrey was wearing a lovely costume. It had long blue feathers coming out of a sparkly swimsuit to make a tail, and a glittering headdress of even more feathers. I thought she looked wonderful, but Auntie Grace didn't.

'It's a fancy-dress gala, over at the Sands Club,' said my mother.

'And what do you think you are supposed to be?' said Grace.

'We're going as Two Lovebirds in a Gilded Cage. My friend Tony made the costumes, aren't they marvellous?' She did a twirl, making Grace even crosser.

Grace was my father's aunt. A tall, stiff woman with a plain but kindly face, she had lived all her life with her brother, Uncle Phil, in a small house in nearby Crosby. I was the only child in their quiet, modest lives, and they tried to love and protect me as best they could. Their house had tall pampas grasses in a jar on the stairs and horse brasses round the fire. On Sundays my mother would drop me off there, and we had lunch in the bare dining room, or on cold days by the living-room fire on a little table. They always gave me my favourite pink and yellow cake with some tinned peaches.

Phil was a trim man with military bearing, and he had his hobbies, which were music and motoring. He loved classical music, and went regularly to the Liverpool Philharmonic, and to his local Gramophone Society, carrying his much-loved gramophone records in a special case with a tweedy cover. After lunch he would play these records for me. It was quite boring, but they were both always so pleased to see me, and there was such a cosy feeling about these visits, that I looked forward to them all week.

Outside our house on my birthday night was a big van, into which my mother disappeared with a wave, but before

Grace.

it could drive off Grace marched up to the passenger seat and that was when there were 'words'. I had been told to get into the car, where Uncle Phil and I now sat, straining to catch the sound of the angry voices.

Grace stomped back to the car and got in; I'd never seen her so cross.

'As per usual, off gallivanting with one of her chaps. Two Lovebirds in a Gilded Cage – that takes the biscuit. They've got it in there, great big thing with a swing inside it, and wheels.'

'What are the swing and wheels for?' I was dying to know.

'Something about her sitting on the swing, and the whole contraption gets wheeled into the party. I've never seen anything so ridiculous in all my life,' Grace said with awful contempt, although I could see that Uncle Phil was quite interested.

'Please can I go and look?' I begged.

I was dying to see the cage on wheels, but was told to stay in the car. Grace said crossly that my mother had told her that she was 'overreacting'.

She told Phil, in a voice that meant I wasn't to hear, 'She said that Tony, the other "lovebird", is the window dresser at Marshall and Snelgrove department store, so there obviously wasn't going to be any funny business. As if that made it all right. I suppose she meant he was, you know, one of those!'

Uncle Phil nodded, but he wasn't a man to get involved. I couldn't resist.

'One of what?' I pleaded.

'Never mind, Sally, it's not very nice,' she said quickly.

In the car she was still whispering but I could hear from the back 'every single night' and 'where does she go to' and 'leaving Sally with total strangers' and 'what poor Neil is suffering'.

I'd seen nothing wrong with my mother going out each night until I realized how upset and angry Grace was, and that my mother's absence wasn't what was expected of a woman with a small child and dying husband.

A sense of unease now hung over the birthday outing, and my excitement of being at the Odeon Cinema at night couldn't quite overcome it. I can remember standing for the National Anthem and doing the Brownies' honour salute, which I had learnt from another girl and would do, even though I wasn't allowed to be a Brownie. I remember the lights dimming and the interval with the usherettes and ice cream and the thrill of being out at night-time mingling with some other anxious feeling I couldn't name.

When we went back to the house it felt darker than usual. Grace led me up the stairs to my room and waited while I put on my nightie and dressing gown, then tucked me in. I asked if I could show Daddy my present she had given me, a painting you could make by filling in the numbered shapes on the black velvet with thick glowing paints. It added up to a picture of a rose, and she told me that 'a red rose means I love you'. Now she said that I'd better not go into Daddy's room, but I could do the painting for him and he could keep it next to his bed.

I had been into his room when he was very ill, so didn't understand why I couldn't go in now. The next day I carefully painted the rose for him, and that night I sat on his bed and gave it to him. He told me that if there was ever a time when he wasn't there, I should remember that his love for me was always with me. Even if I couldn't see it, I could wrap it around me like a big invisible cloak and it would always keep me warm. He said that it would be there for the rest of my life.

I WAS SEVEN YEARS OLD when the afternoon came. I was picked up from school by the mother of a distant cousin, Tracey, which was unusual.

On most mornings I would be collected by a kindly taxi driver my mother had found called Mr Moore, who would then wait by the school gates to drive me home again at the end of the day. Today there was no Mr Moore, only Tracey and her mother.

For me at the time it was just another horrid school day: unremarkable in that I found so many of them miserable. At the age of four I had been put into a small private nursery and primary school called Saxenholme, which was run from a Victorian house rather like the one we lived in, and just as gloomy. I wore something called a 'jibbah' with a big shield on the front, almost as big as me. I dreaded going, and had a daily nervous tummy ache. Even when we were going to make things out of colourful felt, like a flower-basket pin cushion for Mummy, I would look forward to the event, hoping it would cheer me up and asking her surreptitiously, 'Mummy, do you ever use pins?' to which she replied that she did, but when the day came I soon realized that I felt just as unhappy, and things would seem even worse. Then I knew that if I mentioned my tummy ache I could get out of going to school at all. Mr Moore would be standing by his car, dressed smartly in his suit and tie, at half past eight prompt. The housekeeper would appear on the steps and tell him that I was unwell, and, to my enormous relief, he would drive away without me.

If only it had been Mr Moore who was waiting for me on this afternoon three years later. By now I was at the main schoolhouse, having moved when I was five. It had stained glass that made a pattern on the floors, and a smell of bees-wax, chalk and horrible lunches. I dreaded lunch, particularly cheese pie or chocolate sponge, which made me sick. You were allowed to ask for a 'dolly's helping' which I would plead for to the dinner ladies, but the cheesy mush that smelt of vomit was still piled on my plate. I would be left alone in the dining room afterwards with the cold heap in front of me and a teacher looking in to see if I had eaten it yet.

At playtime we went into a back garden that smelt of privet and mulching horse-chestnut leaves. The girls made dens under the trees and, when no one would let me in, I made a broom of twigs and went around saying that I was a sweeper of dens, and offering to sweep for them. No one seemed to want a sweeper and there was a feeling of panic and being unable to breathe, and I would long for the bell to ring so that the lonely feeling could end.

The head teacher, Mrs Jane, was kind and pretty. She would tell us to pull our shoulders back and called us her 'Saxenholme Smarties'. These days she also argued a lot with my mother, who would not let me go swimming in case my hair got wet. Mrs Jane had even offered to dry my hair herself in her study with her own hairdryer. This happened once, but after that my mother got her way by just not sending me to school on swimming days.

Mrs Jane saw my misery and also tried to help me find a friend. One was a girl called Lydia Holroyd whose father had died and all her hair had fallen out. There was one heartbreaking afternoon when her mother picked us up and took me home with them. Lydia seemed very upset that her mother had made a pudding called junket that she hated and when some of it fell onto the carpeted floor her mother scraped it up back into the bowl, slapped her and made her eat it, although it was now covered in fluff and Lydia was crying. Afterwards at school she wouldn't look at me, and we never talked to each other again.

There was another girl who also didn't have a friend. Janet Bailey's father had been blinded during the war and Janet was terribly shy, and was also losing her sight, although my mother thought this was strange as her father's disability was a war wound. She wore very thick glasses and hardly spoke, but if I gave her 'lines' to say, she would say them, and then I could reply and we could play. The awful sad feeling I had at school began to wear off. I dreaded it a little less knowing that I would have my own friend at playtime. But this relief was to be short-lived.

ON THAT PARTICULAR Tuesday I left the old building under swirling skies and scanned the roadside for Mr Moore. He was nowhere to be seen. Instead beyond the rattling fence stood a vaguely familiar Hillman Minx with its doors wide open like traps. It was Tracey and her mother. Why they should be waiting was a mystery, when Tracey was clearly not interested in having me to her house, or even playing with me. She had always stuck to her best friend Debbie Underwood, the most popular girl in class. Since starting school I'd had a strange feeling towards Debbie Underwood. I wanted to be her, but also hated her. Not only did everyone want to be her friend, but she looked like a sunflower with her yellow hair and coltishly long legs. She had a brother, and nice parents, and once told me that she always spent the summer in Appleby.

Summers were my worst time, and although I hated school I dreaded the holidays more, as I would be stuck in the gloomy house while everyone else went away. Visions of Debbie would rise before me. Even the lovely name, Appleby, conjured images of orchards, their trees laden with rosy apples and the long grass studded with daisies. Here golden, long-legged children ran happily in the evening sunshine, a dog at their heels, as they made their way home for a jolly tea.

But on this day everyone, including Tracey, was being kind to me. And there was something suspicious about Tracey's mummy putting so much Matey bubble bath into our night-time bath; even Tracey seemed to find it surprising, and was quickly shushed when she asked about so many special treats.

It was my mother's arrival the next morning that made me realize something was very wrong. It was time for school, but instead of leaving we all went to sit down in the living room where she said she had something sad to tell me: my daddy had died.

Everyone seemed to be looking at me. Only minutes before I had stolen an aniseed ball that I found on top of a cupboard in Tracey's room and popped into my mouth. Now there was an awkward feeling of not knowing what to do with it, or how to spit it out. I remember the taste changing from nice to nasty, as my insides began to fall away. Since then, anything flavoured with aniseed has made me feel sick.

We travelled to school in a convoy. The stained glass in the hall looked weird, the patterns it made on the wall, and the usual everyday sounds of school seemed echoey and far away. Nothing looked as it had the day before. My mother went to see Mrs Jane. At morning assembly Mrs Jane announced that my father had passed away and we would all say a little prayer. I felt faint and as if I wasn't there.

No one took me to the funeral. I had a terrified feeling that I didn't know where Daddy was, or even when he had died. I realized I hadn't seen him for a while, and I felt that during that time he had drifted away because I wasn't there to help him. But surely something so enormous, the end of the world, that changed things for ever, must have been marked by some moment in particular? Instead there were just days that didn't feel right, and then he had vanished from the house. His room was empty, but that wasn't when he died. I hadn't said goodbye. Why hadn't they told me? How had something so earth-shattering happened without my knowing?

Soon after, my mother started saying we would get out of 'this bloody town'. She wrote letters to slight acquaintances, wartime friends, people met in a London nightclub, sent to barely legible addresses from the backs of envelopes. There was no plan, but a vague sense that these 'contacts' could become points on a map that we only had to join to build a yellow brick road to Oz.

But my father was not in Oz. Surely he was somewhere here? I had terrible bad dreams about where his body had gone. One I had over and over involved a room with a high window in an internal wall, and another room the other side of the window where he is lying; but the window is too high and there is nothing to stand on, so I can't look. A rag-and-bone cart arrives in the street, like the one in *Steptoe and Son*, and some men go to the room and take him away, but

I can't get to him. I run out to see the cart moving off down the street with his broken body thrown on top of a heap of bodies, like plague victims from the Black Death. I try to run after it but I can't keep up and feel panic and desperation.

One good memory I had that I would replay in my mind, even though it made me want to howl, was of him peeling grapes for me. They were in a bowl with ice cream, but I hadn't wanted to eat them as I didn't like the skin. So he peeled them with his thin weak hands, using his little bit of strength to make me something to eat. I had wanted him to stop and rest. I kept picturing his sad, kind face as he peeled those grapes.

Some of my mother's letters to 'contacts', which it seemed she may as well have stuffed into bottles and thrown out to sea, had actually begun to drift ashore. Replies came back. Not yet a yellow brick road's worth, but we at least had a safe first stop: my mother's godmother, Auntie Sadie, in New York. She had played a large part in the early drama of Audrey's life and seemed to her a good starting point for a new chapter.

For me it would mean leaving my father behind. The night after hearing he was dead I had watched the news on television, waiting for them to get to the part about him. When he wasn't mentioned I wondered if he would appear the next night, or the next.

By now I felt I would probably hear no more.

One morning we simply marched our baggage past his bare, still room and down the hall.

7

America, 1965

HOT WIND BLOWS across the tarmac to the sound of dying jet engines, the towers of Manhattan in the distance and the sweltering sidewalks of Jackson Heights. 'Hot enough to fry an egg on,' my mother says and I try to picture this and work out if anyone really does it, as we drag our bags along the street. I have heard so many of my mother's tales of America, that it is like a magic land, and I look around in wonder.

In Auntie Sadie's diner there is a counter, and we sit with our bare legs sticking to the hot red leather stools and wait for her to finish pouring someone's coffee. Neat in her waitress uniform, bustling with excitement at our arrival, telling the whole diner, 'From England! My god-daughter, Audrey, and her little girl.'

She hands over keys to the apartment and squeezes me, stroking my pigtails and saying, 'Just like her mother at this age,' while telling my mum, 'You look a million dollars! Mike's getting off early, he's so excited. Leave the bags downstairs, he'll fetch them. I'll be back to make us dinner.

Oh, just look at you!' Her customers watch us; her regulars, they've been hearing of nothing else for weeks.

My mother says we are just stopping over here while she visits some old haunts: 'Then we are off to really see the world.'

Walking up tall stairs we pass so many doors that it feels like a hotel. There is a sweet smell of bubblegum in the hot air. The apartment isn't as I imagined: like the ones in American movies and TV shows, where Lucille Ball comes into a huge living room, tripping over lots of shopping bags.

This is much smaller, but it has a cocktail bar in the living room with tall stools around it. Uncle Mike comes home and lifts me onto a bar stool, saying, 'How about a Shirley Temple?', a fizzy drink which bursts on my tongue and has a sweet cherry stabbed through with a pretty paper umbrella.

He keeps repeating, 'Sadie is just over the moon, over the moon.'

Mike has a splendid red and purple uniform for his job as a hotel doorman. He shows us a framed photograph on the wall, of him standing just behind Richard Nixon, the president. He says, 'You meet all kinds of people in my job, but that really was something.'

Auntie Sadie has tired feet, which she rubs when she gets home and swaps her shoes for little slippers with a marabou pom-pom. She makes dinner with a pudding called Jell-O and my mum picks it up and wobbles it, saying, 'Well, that has to be Jell-O cos jam don't shake like that,' which was a TV advert she saw the last time she visited Sadie before she had me. Then she acts out some other funny adverts, taking

Uncle Mike's hat and putting it on her head to pretend she is strolling along a street, saying, 'Hey, if you want to get ahead, get a hat!'

Sadie and Mike laugh a lot, and get all the photos of my mum out of the drawer. They have been carefully put into big albums with floral covers, unlike the jumble in my mother's box. Many are familiar, but I love hearing the stories again with different details. After dinner, Sadie plays us a little record she has, a recording of my mother aged twenty, being interviewed in New York for a radio show called *Queen for a Day*. I know this story, but my mother sounded so different on the record, it seems like long ago. She was telling the host that she has come all the way from Liverpool. The host says things like, 'How about that!' and 'That's quite a journey.'

'Wait,' says Sadie, holding her hand out, 'now listen to this, it's coming up now!' The host then asks my mother how she's liking New York and she says, 'It's a beautiful city. I'm staying in Jackson Heights with my godmother, Sadie; she sent me the ticket to come to America. It was a birthday gift.'

Sadie looks around at us, delighted. 'My name, on the radio!'

Then the host says, 'So that makes her a real fairy godmother! Did she give you three wishes too? We hope you are going to tell us what those wishes are because *Queen for a Day* is all about making princesses' wishes come true.' Finally he announces that *Queen for a Day* is brought to you by Hartz Mountain Cat Yummies on Mutual Radio Network.

Sadie looks at us again, thrilled. Mike says he's surprised the record hasn't worn out, she's played it that many times! Then it goes on, and my mother tells the host that, if she had three wishes, one would be to visit Clark Gable in Hollywood and the second would be to see all forty-eight states of America. Audrey is about to tell the host what her third wish is when Sadie jumps up and quickly pulls the needle off the record. Mike exchanges a worried look with Sadie, who pats my mother's knee.

'There, we knew you were a Queen from the very day you were born.'

I ask what my mother's third wish was going to be and Sadie hurriedly starts talking about something else.

I felt that the third wish was to do with something unhappy, another piece of my mother's story. There were sections of a jigsaw that were beginning to slot together and make a big picture and, if I could just see it all, this whole thing spread out, then a lot of things would make sense.

In the morning the kitchen is hot and bright, and breakfast is cornflakes with little dried strawberries that puff up when you pour on milk, and Aunt Jemima pancakes with maple syrup. We all sit close together on little stools at the bright yellow Formica table with the sun pouring in and a fan turning to keep us cool.

Then Sadie and Mike go off to work, and my mother sits with her iced coffee. I ask her, 'Tell me again about when you first wanted to come to America.'

'It was during the war,' she begins, and I know that she's in the right mood and wants to remember.

'We couldn't believe it, Jean and I, that there were all these Americans in our town; it was so exciting and we longed to outshine the other girls. We would have a Fred Astaire record spinning on the turntable, and we'd push Jean's bedroom furniture aside to clear a space for us to dance.'

My mother jumps up to demonstrate, humming a tune, and then, waiting for the beat, she clicks her fingers. 'It was suddenly all jive talk like, "OK you kool kat, you a boogie-man? Then let's have a clambake," which meant let's have a jive session.'

I loved her doing the jive talk.

'Here goes – kick, ball, change, walk, walk.' She swings her hips, knees bent, and sings along as she dances the 'Shorty George . . .' Then you have to get your hips swinging; Jean would be dancing too as I taught her all the moves and I'd say, "Yeah, that's it, dancin' lady, you've got it!"'

'And why did so many American people come to South-port?' We only knew one American there now, a lady called Mitzi whose husband made cars and who my mother and Auntie Ava talked about because of her Texan accent and her trouser suits.

'We were lucky. Of course the war was terrible and Liver-pool was being badly bombed, but Southport was far enough away from it all, and we had a much easier war than most places. Then, suddenly in 1942, these hundreds of American boys and men arrived, from the South, from Midwest farms, young ones and old ones, though mostly young. The Palace Club was full of them, and so was the town.'

Mum aged 17.

Southport's Palace Hotel, not far from our house, had once been one of the grandest and biggest in Britain. People talked about it having a thousand rooms, billiard halls, croquet on the lawns, stables, evening concerts, orchestral teas and dancing; it even had its own railway station and air landing strip. Then it had been taken over by the American Red Cross and now 'the Palace Club' it was one of their largest rest and recreation centres in Britain for bomber crews from the US Air Force. More than fifteen thousand airmen came to recuperate there, or to take a break between their bombing raids over Europe.

Mum, left, with Sadie, Southport sea front.

Jean had volunteered as a wireless telegraphist and was now away training all week. Audrey was keen to do something for the war effort, but didn't want to abandon her mother and her new life in the town. The Palace Club was in urgent need of young lady hostesses to welcome the airmen, serve the teas and chat to them as they sat on the verandah taking the 'sea air'. Audrey was just seventeen when she signed up for what shifts she could manage, and was soon drawn into a whole new gloriously shiny world.

At home she and her mother scraped by on rations like everyone else, so she marvelled at the club's 'All You Can Eat' snack bar with Coca-Cola and fresh doughnuts, both highly exotic and unavailable anywhere else in wartime Britain. To Audrey, the American men were just as exotic in their crisp uniforms, so well cut and in a beautiful-quality cloth, utterly unlike the cheap rough serge the British lads were given. They had an immediate glamour as they stood around the pool tables, chewing gum or playing baseball on the lawns outside.

At the dances, held there three times a week, a live band played swing, bebop and jazz and Audrey was delirious with pleasure as the airmen swung her around the floor to the new American dance music that transported her to another planet. The dark days of the war had drained the colour out of British daily life, but here on her doorstep was a piece of amazing Technicolor America. She was already imagining more than her childhood dreams ever encompassed, and who knew who, or what, would be her ticket to this brilliant future? Above all, she wanted love – epic, sweeping, and passionate, the kind of love that she now lay awake at night aching for. She scanned the faces of the young men at the club, with their eager shining eyes, but they seemed such boys, and she was imagining a manly man, who would sweep her up into this new life.

Then something happened that was beyond even her more fantastic dreams.

It is a hot summer's day in 1943 and Audrey is arriving for her shift when a jeep roars up, passing her on the driveway of the Palace Hotel Red Cross Centre, and out jump two men in air-force uniform. Quickly one of the men holds up a film camera to his eye and is pointing and following every move of his buddy. His buddy is handsome, very handsome, with dark features and a grin that altogether seems oddly familiar. As the news spreads up into the hotel and staff begin running about in a frenzy of excitement, she realizes that this is the long-rumoured visit that no one had ever believed would happen. This is a real-life visit from Hollywood star Clark Gable.

She had seen him not long before as the reckless adventurer in *Gone With the Wind*, sweeping Scarlett O'Hara off her feet, and she was a passionate fan, along with millions of other women. Not only was he the biggest star of his day, known as 'the King', but he had also made several trips flying in dangerous combat missions over Europe so he was now a hero outside of the screen. The crew was there making *Combat America* about the American war effort, and to film Gable meeting the convalescing airmen at the Palace Club.

Audrey pushed her way through the crowd standing on the terrace to watch Gable and his entourage, and she saw that he was chatting to the matron and assembled dignitaries. She stepped forward with a cheeky 'Hello!', her hand held out towards Gable, as if she was part of this awkward welcoming committee and the one who was meant to liven things up. The manager and matron were too taken aback by her sudden appearance to stop her.

Gable shook her hand politely.

'Welcome to Southport, Riviera of the North West!' she said with a wry smile.

'Well, that's quite a claim!' He grinned back at her.

Mum, 1943.

'I think you'll find we live up to it. When you've seen the Palace here, you should look around the town.'

'And what does it offer the visitor beside fish and chips and warm beer?' he laughed.

'Well, Napoleon loved it so much he built Paris after it and –' hardly pausing for breath '– then there is the Sea Bathing Lake, the Pleasure Gardens, and the pier's got its own railway so you can take a train right out to the sea . . .' So, there and then, Audrey was invited along to join him and the crew the next day. They were going to be filming a tour of the town as a Hay Ride, complete with pony and trap.

Despite his success, Gable was in some ways still a boy from the oil fields of Ohio. The next day, as they waited for the crew to set up, he and Audrey chatted and he asked her about her life and talked of where he grew up. Audrey saw him just as he was, and the only sign of Rhett Butler was a big wink he gave her at intervals throughout the day, the white teeth gleaming in his grin. His job complete, they said goodbye and, as he was leaving, Audrey told him, 'One day I'm going to make it to America,' and he said the fatal words, 'Well, be sure to look me up if you do!'

He had gone, leaving her dizzy with the memory. She had been going home every night with her pockets stuffed full of scraps of paper with scribbled addresses from Idaho to Alabama and pleas from the men to 'come visit me some day!' and now, not only had hundreds of young handsome Americans practically fallen for her, but her favourite movie star had just walked into her life too and as good as invited her to visit him in Hollywood. Her fantasies about getting out of the grind of dirty old Bootle to Southport had suddenly been dwarfed by the idea of America.

So, here we were all these years later. Even the way she said the word, 'America', with a thrill in her voice, had made me want to come here too. But now that we were here I realized that this was more than just a visit; it seemed that we were on some kind of quest, or mission. We were at the start of this adventure, but how it related to all these past stories was as yet unknown.

8

The Kill Devil Hills

THE REST OF THE TIME in New York was a blur of wonders. Sadie and Mike swept us off to Coney Island, the
World Fair and other places that made America feel like
another planet, although their little apartment felt more and
more like home. The area around my bed filled with presents
and souvenirs. They hugged me all the time and called me
'angel cake' and 'honey bun'. Sadie did my hair in a pretty
style called a French pleat, and gave me slides and something
called bandeaux in lots of colours to match my clothes. They
didn't want us to leave. But my mother wanted to 'get on',
although I didn't know what we were getting on with, or
where we were going.

Finally, however, we left New York after a few weeks,
through a mist of tears: mine and Sadie's. My mother tried
to pretend she was sorry to leave but her excitement at the
next adventure was obvious, even if the adventure itself was
a mystery to the rest of us. 'Let's get this show back on the
road!' was all she'd say. She didn't like to be asked questions.
When I tried her with, 'What was your third wish when you

were Queen for a Day?' she just didn't answer. She could have said she didn't remember or something, but instead she would just ignore me so that I knew not to ask again.

THE GREYHOUND BUS took a whole long day to reach North Carolina. My mother had said we were going to Kitty Hawk, a name that made you think of desert rocks and hawks and Native American landscapes. She had said it quickly, 'Kitty Hawk, Kildevil Hills', which made it sound rather exciting.

Then Uncle Mike had found it on the map, and showed me that the place was really called Nag's Head, and it was right by the Kill Devil Hills, between the Alligator River and something known as the Great Dismal Swamp. There wasn't one single lovely word in there anywhere. My mother promised me that there was a beach, and that she had a job in a nice hotel with a pool where I could play, but somehow, looking out of the bus window, I couldn't feel anything but fearful.

Long hours went by as we travelled, and I couldn't even read my book as it made me feel sick on the swaying bus.

I begged my mother to tell me a story, one I'd never heard before, and she sighed.

'Well, OK, here is one. When I was growing up there was a girl who lived near us called Mary, a sweet-faced little thing who we always felt sorry for because she came from such a big, rough family. Auntie Sadie was fond of her, and when Mary's sixteenth birthday came round, Sadie offered to take her to the big department store in Liverpool where Sadie worked as a waitress, and to buy Mary a fancy tea there.'

'At Lewis's?' I knew the store.

'Yes, that's right.' She carried on:

'Then, after Sadie and Mary had eaten their tea, and said their goodbyes, Mary suddenly realized that she had left her bag behind and had to go back into the store all alone.

'The staff sent her up to the Lost and Found desk, and when Mary arrived there she found a smartly dressed older gentleman talking to the girl who worked at the desk; so the girl then went off to look for the package that the man had lost.

'While the girl was away, the man, perhaps thinking he was alone, gave a deep sigh, but then he turned to notice Mary waiting behind him. He began to chat to her, and, discovering that it was her birthday, he warmly wished her many happy returns.

'After a while the girl who worked there came back with his lost package and handed it to him. He looked at it rather wistfully, then turned to Mary, holding out the parcel. "My dear, I'd like you to accept this small gift from me, along with my wishes for many more happy birthdays. I imagine you are a more worthy recipient than the lady it was intended for, and hope that life treats you kindly in the years to come."

'With that he rushed away, before Mary even had a chance to speak or thank him, and she stood there holding the package in astonishment.'

My mother paused.

'What was it?' I asked eagerly, and she smiled.

'Mary unwrapped the paper and inside was a box which she opened. Inside *that*, on a velvet cushion, glittered a small heart-shaped brooch.

'The girl who worked there took it from her and read the label. "That's a proper diamond there, that is!" she said jealously.

'Mary gazed at the gift; it was so much more beautiful than anything she had ever imagined owning. She kept the brooch all her life and wore it on her wedding day, and it always made her feel special.'

I smiled. 'That was a nice story. Wasn't she lucky?'

'I suppose she was,' sighed my mother, 'but you can't wait for Lady Luck to just appear. You could wait an awfully long time at the Lost and Found desk without any diamonds turning up, don't you think?'

After that she closed her eyes, and I wondered if she was asleep.

At last we arrived in Nag's Head. The air outside the bus was sweltering and there were no taxis, only a very grumpy man who said he would have to go a long way out of his way to drive us to where we were going.

My mother had this idea that asking people to help you was actually an act of kindness in itself, as it made them feel good about themselves. Ideally you found a really bad-tempered, unhelpful person to help you, then you praised them lavishly, telling them how generous and wonderful they were; this would make them feel suddenly happier and more inclined to help someone else in future. So her theory went, but it had already let us down once or twice.

84

I was relieved to see that this time it had worked and, after struggling with all our bags in the heat, the man cheered up under the warm glow of her thanks and her enormous interest in his truck, and we all made our way to the Kitty Hawk Motel, which was near the Kitty Hawk Museum of Aviation, but felt like it wasn't really anywhere at all.

The town we were in was hardly a town, just a big road in an America which I had begun to realize had miles and miles of big roads and towns that hardly anyone visits. This one had a petrol station and a hardware store with a bench for coffee and drinks.

Along the highway was the motel and diner, owned by a lady called Diane Johnson; my mother had met her one weekend and kept her address for nearly twenty years. Diane was very suntanned, wore tight trousers and sunglasses and looked tired. She acted pleased to see us but didn't talk to me very much. She admitted that not many people came here. A handful came to visit the museum, which was at the place from where the Wright Brothers flew the first aeroplane. We climbed up the steep hill one morning through the hot thick air only to find that it was hardly a museum at all, more of a monument and rest area with a few outdoor plaques. It wasn't surprising that visitors here were usually on the way to somewhere else, and there wasn't much reason to overnight except being too exhausted to get to the next place.

So why were we here?

'Three questions,' my mother would say, holding up those three fingers, but I only got an answer if they were silly things, about things that didn't really matter.

'Why are we in this dull place?' That would have been the first.

The second would be 'And why were you here once before?' – for my mother had been before to this place, and even this very motel. This made it more unforgivable that she'd brought us here and made it sound so much better. Even the promised swimming pool at the motel was very small and hot and in a car park. The first time I swam my shoulders were so pink and burnt I didn't go in again.

The third question would be 'When can we leave?'

But I was beginning to learn that this would never get an answer and that our moving on had an entirely secret logic that would never be explained.

The only thing that broke up the appalling boredom was a chambermaid called Fay whom I adored, with lovely skin and a purring way of talking. Fay would let me 'help' her make motel beds and clean rooms and tell me about her boyfriend and her jealous sister who was a little on the 'heavy' side and didn't go to work. But even Fay didn't seem to feel she would be stuck there much longer and talked about moving to the city. When Fay clocked off the rest of the day yawned terrifyingly empty. The motel had nowhere to explore and everything had the same bubblegum smell of America; outside was too hot to bear. My mother helped in reception, handing out keys to the occasional visitor and writing letters to people. When they weren't working she and Diane sat at a table talking quietly.

It was here that I became frightened for the first time, frightened that we could get stuck somewhere that didn't even quite seem to exist.

There was a road that led down to a beach and sand dunes, but it was so stifling that nobody went down there. The beach had a pier, but it didn't have the things that Southport pier had, like amusement arcades and a miniature railway. This was just a long wooden deck. We walked along it once when the intense daytime heat had given way to a damp evening heat that still made dribbles of sweat run down your face. There were two men fishing at the end.

We then walked along the boardwalk, past the sand dunes to a shabby building on the beach with a big sign saying NAG'S HEAD CASINO and some faded posters for entertainers who were performing there. My mother had been here before. She said it had felt quite different then. She had visited the place once 'with some people I was working with'.

It was closed now, and we had just started to walk back along the beach when my mother began crying and couldn't stop. We sat by the dunes, and the sand was still baking although the sun had gone down. Question Three: 'Why are you so sad?' She cried and cried, but I knew she wouldn't tell me what the matter was. In the end I was weeping too, because she wouldn't tell me. I had no sense of what could have brought her to this place long before I was born.

A FEW DAYS LATER we met someone called George who drove out to see us. He was one of my mother's conquests from the Palace Club. Back then he was a romantic figure bravely dealing with painful injuries suffered when his plane had crashed over France. George now had a farm miles away, and his wife had died recently. My mother had learnt this

George c.1943.

from the Christmas cards they had exchanged each year since their brief wartime meeting. She told me that George had been left with a son named Danny, and his wife's mother had moved in to cook and help them. He took Audrey out to a restaurant somewhere for a meal, then he dropped her back, and the visit seemed to have gone well. As he left a plan was made that we would go to stay with him the following week.

After he'd gone she seemed happy and sang me all the songs from a musical called *Oklahoma!*, and taught me how to dance at a hoedown, telling me all about square dances and what fun they were and how we would probably go to one.

On his next visit George drove us out to his house for a weekend. It took hours and my mother was nervous, fidgeting and talking about all kind of things as George became quieter and quieter. When we finally got there I met George's son, Danny, who was fourteen and seemed shy, and we all had a dinner that my mother said was 'real American home cooking'. Danny showed me how to put the corncob holders into the ends of the corn and brush the melted butter on before we ate it. I liked him, and the comfortable farmhouse kitchen though I somehow could feel that my mother was terribly disappointed in it all.

The weekend felt too long. Danny and I watched TV in the living room and played with his dog. At last it was time to drive us back to Kitty Hawk. George said even less this time, and my mother had never been so quiet, for she must have told him every one of her thousand and one stories already. After George dropped us back she stood outside in the terrible heat and looked bleakly out at the freeway and the billboards and the huge fields beyond them and said, 'I think we'd better go.' Was that why we were here? Had she thought she might love George and then found that she didn't?

'Was George why we came here?'

'No, it was all about something that happened a long time ago, before you were born.'

When she looked at me I knew that she wished I wasn't a child, that she wanted me to just get on with growing up.

Of course, I knew more than she thought. She tried to keep her secrets, and to protect me from the adult world, but she was a helpless storyteller, and, like all children, I was a brilliant secret listener, hovering by open doorways or, even if I was right beside her, adept at appearing to be deep in my book, while actually absorbing every detail of what was being said. So it was unlikely that any stories involving 'Love', this being my particular study, would slip by me unnoticed.

I already knew, therefore, that in that same year, and in the same spot that she had shaken the hand of Clark Gable, something had happened that changed everything. All her dreams had evaporated. She had fallen in love for the first time. I had heard her tell the story.

9

True Love

JAMES LEADSOM was in RAF uniform that day, when he came to visit a friend of his who was convalescing at the Palace Club. Audrey always remembered her first sight of him walking towards her down a corridor. Love just comes calling, and it isn't a war hero or a film star, she now discovered. It is just a boy. And time – and she said that she always remembered this curious effect – really did stop dead still. Now it hit, and all the clichés she had heard about were suddenly true. Everything around her really did seem to melt away, as if she were in a tunnel where everything was invisible except for this boyishly handsome face, with its floppy blond hair falling across his deep blue eyes. She went in search of him, then found him at his friend's bedside and introduced herself.

That night she lay in bed, terrified to think that these feelings might vanish, that it might have all been an illusion. What if she met James again and those feelings were not there? Then Sunday, the fateful day, came and they were to meet at the station. He'd be wearing his 'civvies' to take her to tea, and all the girls had talked about the moment they

James Leadsom.

saw their men out of uniform and found that the magic had gone. For Audrey, though, as she walked towards him, she knew immediately that the feelings were stronger than ever. His willowy grace and long legs made him look just as good in his slouchy well-worn cords and baggy sweater, and he was strong and sweet, as excited about life as she was, and she was crazy about him.

It was the shock that would turn everything upside down for my mother. Her drive to escape the darkness of that life in Liverpool had been fuelled by a fantasy – but of what exactly? Where was this magical kingdom she was heading for, and who was this man who would take her there? It was still a small girl's dream of a prince, not a pauper.

Now she was faced with the reality, that love comes to find you, whether you like it or not, and it may be in the shape of a young man with modest ambitions, offering you a cosy home, a family, just one plain and simple dream rather than the myriad that might be fluttering around in your head. None of this had ever occurred to her.

James had one simple plan: to work at his father's business and to raise a family in the village of nearby Formby where he himself had spent his own happy childhood. James, as madly in love with Audrey as she was with him, was quick to propose marriage. Peace was now in the air and there was an expectation that the war would be over soon. James was to leave the RAF and start work, and they would be married. She of course said yes; before his leave ended she was already wearing an engagement ring. What happened next was a big missing piece of her story, but she had stopped here.

'I'll tell you about it all one day,' she now promised.

'So it was Auntie Sadie who went to America then, wasn't it?' I asked, drawing her out.

'Yes, we all thought Sadie wouldn't marry. All the girls were falling for the Americans, and Sadie had lots of suitors but never went for anyone. Then Mike came along, "a determined Yankee" as he called himself. I liked him straight away, I like those fast-talking New Yorkers, and he had an easy laugh and a big heart. That Christmas he got some leave and headed back to claim her as his bride.'

I knew the photograph that had been taken outside the Registry Office on Lord Street showing an odd group. Mike stands in his uniform, looking proud, with one arm around his bride, Sadie, who looks anxious, and the other arm around my nana, Rebecca, who looks faded and tired. The other women wear serviceable wartime coats, and only Audrey has a huge fur hat and matching muff, and is grinning away as if it was her own wedding.

Then the war had ended, and in May 1945 Audrey and Nana gathered with the crowds on Lord Street to hear the King's speech for VE Day in London. Hundreds of servicemen and women paraded by to a marching band as the crowd, swathed in Union Jacks, cheered. But I knew that all Audrey could think of, night and day, was James. They were planning to go to London as soon as he was demobbed, and she decided to go there to wait for him. She hated to desert her mother, but knew that she and James would have a freedom in the big city that they wouldn't have at home.

She found the post-war life of Southport deadly, as the airmen all left the town and the local shops shut at five o'clock. She always loved what she called 'night life', and dreaded Sundays and the time when everything closed, declaring it was all 'Dead! Dead! Dead!' and she was 'Bored! Bored! Bored!' So now she took a train to London, found a job in a dry cleaner's and rented a bedsit in Maida Vale on a corner by Warwick Road tube station.

She had pointed it out to me. 'There, my little room was just in that corner. I just had a little gas ring where I lived on powdered eggs and a one-bar electric fire to dry my nylons on. That's where I lost my virginity.' So it all passed into legend, and decades later my own daughter, Molly, aged four, who had overhead the whispers, told an elderly gentleman who we were giving a lift to, 'That's where Nana lost her ginity.'

After the glow of victory had faded, London was revealed as grim, war-torn and desperate. When James was demobbed they spent those few months together exploring the battered city. Rationing was at its worst; there was little food or coal. They cuddled up by the fire in cosy pubs to keep warm, cooking over the gas ring in the bedsit, and making love.

One night she and James had managed to get tickets up in the gods for a show that had been sold out for months, the musical *Oklahoma!* at Drury Lane. After the grey drabness and cold of post-war London the curtain came up on a set blazing with orange and yellow, bringing the British a dazzling vision of the sun of the Great Plains and the vast wheatfields of America. The exuberance of the dancing and upbeat innocence of songs like 'Oh, What a Beautiful Mornin'' contained all the sunshine and energy of a British fantasy of American life. At the end the audience wouldn't let the cast go home, and the actors all came down into the auditorium and sang every single song again, with the crowd swaying and dancing in the aisles. Audrey never stopped singing the songs, or remembering that night. America was still for her, more than ever, the Promised Land. But she had no possibility of ever getting there, and anyway she was about to become Mrs James Leadsom in only a few months' time.

That Christmas the Formby pinewoods along the beach had a light sprinkling of snow, as James and Audrey walked hand in hand talking about their future. They were home visiting Southport to see the New Year in with family, and were planning to marry in the spring. They had driven out to Formby, where James's parents lived, to look at houses that they might be able to afford. Life as a housewife, with children and a domestic routine, was not something Audrey could easily imagine. It was very different from the fantasies that had filled her head before she met James; now she was so besotted that she simply accepted it all and wandered through the days in a trance.

She returned home to her mother's to say goodbye, just before she and James set off back to London. She found Sadie there in a terrible state of anxiety. Because of the war Sadie had seen nothing of her husband Mike for almost a year, and now she had just heard that he had been sent back to New York. She was clutching his letter, and said that he was asking for her to come to join him in America. In a couple of weeks she was to go and board the buses from Liverpool, with the other war brides, to be taken down to the Southampton docks to set sail. Audrey promised that she would travel down from London to meet Sadie at Southampton and see her off to this new life.

The *Queen Mary* liner had been hastily requisitioned to take nearly two thousand brides to their new lives waiting for them in America. The ship seemed massive, towering over Audrey and Sadie as they stood among the crowds waiting to wave off their loved ones. They had only a few moments before Sadie was herded away. The boat was swarming with women, some holding babies and small children, some leaning out of portholes, as the long mournful horn sounded and the tugs began to take her out to sea.

Standing watching the great ship sail out reawakened Audrey's desire to know more about this vast continent that she was half in love with, from the movies and from the long sighs of the convalescing airmen she had met, pouring out to her their dreams of home. Their descriptions of the bustling snow-covered streets of their hometowns, shining with lights at Christmas time, or the sounds of kids playing baseball on summer nights in the Midwest, all fed her hungry curiosity and she longed to see it all for herself.

The crossing took just over a week, and before long Sadie was sending Audrey and her mother long letters. She enclosed the daily on-board newspaper *Wives Aweigh*, in which she had written an article about the Palace Club and Audrey's day out with Clark Gable. She explained the holes in the newspaper were where she had torn out the recipes for suggested meals to cook for your new husband, including, she said, 'breakfast pancakes, meat loaf and corn fritters'.

Sadie was relieved to find Mike eagerly awaiting her amid the chaos of the Red Cross staff, who were attempting to reunite hundreds of brides with their luggage and husbands. Luckily Mike seemed just the same as ever, and Sadie said she was very happy in her nice little apartment with its modern all-American kitchen, making breakfast pancakes for her all-American husband.

But her most exciting news was that she was now sending Audrey a ticket to join her there for a holiday, and to travel on that very same ocean liner. Mike knew how much Sadie had wanted Audrey to come to see her in her new home, and so he had saved for it, and here it was, along with the latest green nylon stockings that girls were queuing up for and which wouldn't reach Britain for a long time.

Audrey unwrapped the emerald-green stockings, and stared at the ticket feeling torn between powerful excitement and sadness. She only wished the timing had all been different. But when James heard the news he surprised her by encouraging her to go, believing that this would give her just the adventure she needed before they married and started a family. This was an idea that she could hardly resist, although it would be a wrench to be apart from him. She only had the money for a short holiday, and to have at least seen New York would be something; the rest of America would wait.

Her mother travelled with her down to the Southampton docks to see her off. The long tangle of streamers linked those up on the ship's decks with their loved ones waving and weeping down below. A band played, and they arrived to find the gangway crowded with fans and reporters – the actor Rex Harrison was boarding the liner.

Audrey had bought an emerald-green suit and hat to match the new green stockings. She now tapped the photographer of *Illustrated Magazine* on the shoulder.

'Excuse me, I'm a newspaper journalist myself, but I can offer you a bit of a scoop if you are interested?'

'Always interested in a scoop, miss.'

She pointed down to her legs.

'Just something for the ladies, but these happen to be the first green nylons in Britain – another sign that colour is coming back into our lives now that the war is over.'

The picture he took shows her posing beside the gangway with complete confidence, her foot forward in her best beauty-queen pose, as if the surrounding crowds gathered to see off Rex Harrison were really all there just for her. As Harrison turned to look, Audrey called out to him, like an old friend, 'I must say, Rex, I thought *Anna and the King* was divine.'

She kept that copy of the magazine, sent on to New York by her mother, showing herself in a full-page spread with a caption saying, 'The First Girl in Green Nylons – Miss Audrey Miller Boards the *Queen Mary* for New York.' The serendipity of that moment seemed to hint at what was to come. I knew this story well. I longed to know what had happened next, and why she had wept that day at the beach beside the Nag's Head Casino.

10

The Further Adventures
of Audrey

MORE GREYHOUND BUSES, more long roads that stretched
to the horizon, and more stops in bus stations with smelly
toilets and nasty sandwiches, but at least we were leaving the
Kill Devil Hills.

We drove into Los Angeles to stay somewhere that my
mother seemed very excited about, called the Roosevelt
Hotel, which was right in Hollywood. When we arrived it
was disappointing; 'it had gone way downhill' she told me,
and the lobby was now full of young women who were 'ladies
of the night'. She was too scared of the busy streets to try
driving in Los Angeles, and she explained that the place was
'impossible without a car' so we wouldn't be staying long.
But fiddle-de-dee, we would soon be on a bus again anyway,
travelling somewhere else to see a lady called Miss Gillette,
but for now we were here in this place I'd heard so much
about.

We dressed up in our best clothes, made our hair flicky
with Carmen rollers then walked down Hollywood Boulevard together looking swanky. She told me stories about

Grauman's Chinese Theatre, and pointed out the big yellow stars in the pavement and did funny impersonations of the people whose names were written on the slabs. She acted out scenes from films they had been in and people stopped to watch, laughing.

I could tell she was feeling sorry that the Kill Devil Hills had not been much fun for either of us, and she was now trying to make it up to me, so we held hands and sang songs, and she hugged me a lot, calling me Sallylicious and My Poppet. I knew that when she was happy and looking forward to something it was easier for her to love me.

We sat in a fancy restaurant for dinner and, as she was in such a good mood, I asked her, 'Tell me again how you met Miss Gillette?' This was the lady who we were going to see, and I'd only heard fragments of this tale before and never quite joined up the pieces.

'It was on board the ship that I first met her. The ticket that Auntie Sadie had sent me was just tourist class and I was dying to see the really swanky parts of the ship, the First Class restaurants with all the fancy people and lovely ballrooms.

'At night I'd wander the decks, and would see movie stars like Rex Harrison as he smoked a cigarette up on the top deck, but I had no access to go up there.

'Then I made friends with the ship's butcher, as it was his job to walk the First Class doggy passengers on the sports deck each morning, so he knew all the gossip. You learn that as a social columnist – how to find the person with the inside track. So I asked him about the dogs and their owners and made notes about them in my reporter's notebook.

'"Well, this little fluffy one belongs to Miss Gillette – you know, like the razor blades," he told me, and I asked him, "And are the dogs like their owners at all, would you say?"

'"Well, he's a nice little dog, and Miss G is a very nice older lady."'

Matching dogs to their owners became a sport; she waited, chatting to her friend the butcher one day, until Miss Gillette, the razor-blade lady, came to pick up her dog, then Audrey befriended her.

At first the ship had just felt like a floating city, a huge immovable thing past which the ocean rolled, but then out in the Gulf Stream they hit a winter storm. The liner began a slow pitching, and soon many of the passengers disappeared into the cabins feeling unwell. As First Class rapidly emptied, Miss G, who was made of sturdier stuff, found herself deserted by her friends, and so made Audrey her constant companion; together they strolled the more elegant of the lounges and cocktail bars and the lavish ballroom with its nightly orchestra and dances.

Miss G was a rather splendidly handsome woman who had never found a man good enough, and busied herself with gossip and philanthropy. She hosted her legendary lunches in Los Angeles, and loved to name-drop all her famous guests. As the weather improved Audrey continued to spend time with her amusing new friend, who was tough, and had a cutting tongue, but showed Audrey real kindness. Afternoons were spent playing cards with Miss G and her companions in the First Class lounge as they chatted about their well-known acquaintances. One of Miss G's oldest friends in Los

Angeles was Audrey's role model, the gossip columnist Hedda Hopper, and Audrey entertained everyone with a version of the popular song 'A Hat for Hedda Hopper', using whatever was handy to assemble into a funny hat.

Take a table-tennis bat, and here's a crab –
That's quite a whopper!
Add some flowers and what have you got –
It's a hat for Hedda Hopper!

Miss Gillette took a picture of Audrey in one of these creations to show Hedda when she got home, and she made Audrey parade around the whole First Class dining room wearing the crab-shell and bat hat to everyone's amusement. By the time they arrived in America, Audrey's collection of contacts had grown considerably.

In New York a dense fog had descended and the sights that Audrey had crowded on deck to see, the Statue of Liberty and beyond it the skyscrapers of Manhattan, were shrouded in an icy mist. For some time the liner couldn't enter the harbour and Audrey just stood there, pulling her coat tightly around her, as their foghorn and the neighbouring boats wailed to each other across the bay. Then suddenly the ship was on her way, so full of life, as everyone made ready for the arrival. At last, through patchy fog, she saw it, the tall statue looming beside them, holding her lamp aloft and the lights of the city beyond, all twinkling through the winter gloom. She could hardly breathe, it felt so unreal that she was actually here in America.

Crowds waited to greet them on the long balcony overlooking the harbour. Sadie and Mike excitedly pushed their way through to Audrey as she stepped off the ship, waving goodbye to her travel companions.

Sadie and Mike's apartment was not as she had imagined, which was something up among the skyscrapers or overlooking Central Park, but on the corner of a modest block on a side street of a working-class suburb. Every morning of her holiday she would leave early with Mike, who travelled in to his job in a big hotel, and when she emerged into Manhattan she would marvel at 'the Wonder City' as it honked, roared and rushed past her.

Each day she felt more at home, buying the glossy pretzels and malted milk from the street carts, inhaling the New York smells of fresh bagels and salty air blown in from the water. She loved to walk in the deep shadows of the tall buildings and feel the breathless flurry of the crowds all about her, the exhilaration of people as they dashed into doorways, cabs and subway entrances.

'Of course in my fantasies I was in the New York of the movies,' she would say of this time. 'I was off sipping Martini at the Copacabana Bar with Cary Grant, not sitting each night in Mike and Sadie's little apartment with our TV dinners on a tray. But how was I going to change that with only a few dimes in my pocket?'

One day she found herself outside Macy's department store, and saw people crowding in, the air buzzing with excitement. She followed the crush of jostling shoppers to the ballroom, and squeezed through to the front to see what was happening, then watched intently as a line of girls stepped up to audition for a radio show called *Queen for a Day*. She read the flyer saying that one of the prizes was 'Dinner with Your Favorite Movie Star!' When the radio host asked if anyone else wanted to take part, Audrey quickly raised her hand and joined the line.

That evening she decided not to tell Sadie and Mike that she had passed the audition and won a chance to compete in the final the following day. She put on her lucky green suit and stockings and set off with Mike for the city in the morning, although she was jittery with nerves as she made her way back to the Macy's ballroom. The show was a live broadcast and when her time came the hospitality girl counted her in and pushed her forward.

She took a deep breath and stepped up to the podium, telling herself that this wasn't so very different to being lifted onto that kitchen table back in Bootle as a little girl to 'do a turn'. She knew she must give it her full PERSONALITY.

'So, Audrey Miller, why do you want to be Queen for a Day?' the host asked.

She began with the story of her escape from her Bootle childhood, where 'on a Saturday night the streets echoed with all the drunken singing, as I ran for my life when the police saw me coming out of the pub with the bets . . .'

She talked about the sighs of 'those young airmen, who would pour out their dreams of home' as they recovered from their injuries, and of the many invitations she'd been given to come and visit them in cities and farms across America.

Audrey, New York, c.1946.

She described the moment when 'who should jump out of that jeep but Rhett Butler, right in front of me, right out of the movie screen and into real life . . .' to offer her his personal invitation to come and see him too . . . and how she longed to take up that invitation . . .

The applause at the end was heartfelt, as the commentator announced that Miss Audrey Miller was the winner, and the host signed off with, 'This is Jack Bailey, wishing we could make every single woman a Queen, for every single day.'

Louis Jourdan.

Her first excited question was about the prize of dinner with a real movie star, but she was told this did not include a trip to Hollywood to meet Mr Gable. Instead she was offered dinner with a young actor who was here in New York, and given a free makeover to prepare for it. She spent the day being coiffed and groomed in the store's beauty parlour and picked out the perfect black dress with a fishtail, and was given jewellery to wear with it. Then she was taken by limousine to a supper club where a grand dance floor revolved to the sound of a big-band orchestra. She was, for once, almost frozen with nerves as the publicist walked her across to join Louis Jourdan, a handsome young French man at a secluded table.

She soon found that Louis was easy company; he was young and, although he'd just starred in a Hitchcock film, he was still new to the film business. They chatted about their lives, their war experiences, his time in the French Resistance, and his impressions of America. The club had a magician who came over to their table and conjured a red rose from behind her ear, which she later pressed to send in one of her love letters to James. At the end of the evening Louis gave her a signed photograph and wrote on the back the name of the restaurant he had told her about. 'To Audrey, remember – Antoine's in New Orleans, see you there to eat snails! Your friend, Louis!'

Her thoughts of seeing any more of America could only be fantasies, as she knew that she had just enough money to see her through her remaining couple of weeks. She was barely managing on her small amount of savings as it was, and James was waiting.

Then, as the Macy's publicist put her into a car to take her home, she asked Audrey if she wanted to hand over the jewellery, just to keep in the Macy's safe. Up to this moment Audrey had missed the fact that the little diamond pendant at her throat was so valuable. The publicist told her that, if she preferred, she could return it to Macy's and take the cash instead.

The next morning Audrey went into Macy's and was handed a banker's draft for three hundred dollars, a small fortune. Her decision was made in an instant, and in fact was hardly a decision at all. She went to the station and bought a train ticket to Los Angeles. Then she returned to Jackson

Heights, packed her bag and sat down to share all the excitement with James.

> I know, my darling, that you will understand why I
> am staying away for a little longer, before we settle
> down to our wonderful new life together. It will all
> be something to tell our children.

She signed the letter 'your very own Queen for a Day, and soon to be your Queen for ever'.

Sadie and Mike waved her off anxiously, making her promise to send addresses and news from wherever she was.

I liked this story, but I still wanted to know if she had seen Miss G again, after the cruise ship? She was tired and would only say that yes, she had, but she would tell me about that another time.

II

Palm Springs

WE FINALLY TOOK a Greyhound bus through California to meet Miss Gillette who was now very old and lived in a place called Palm Springs. For once somewhere looked like its name, with beautiful homes with soft green lawns, roads lined with tall palm trees and rose coloured mountains in the distance.

We were picked up from the bus station by a chauffeur in uniform called Nick. He was very small and looked just like *My Favorite Martian*, a TV show I liked, and I thought he was very funny. He described himself as Miss G's 'close companion' and when we arrived at the palatial house, where Miss G was in bed, he showed us around proudly as if it was all his own.

He took us through the rooms, telling us about each object, which French Impressionist painted this painting, or how some desk came from 'a real French chateau'. There were stories about how Queen Alexandra had had the tea set commissioned for her trousseau, which Nick explained meant when she got married, but my mother was tired and said afterwards that she could have done without the tour, and that he was nice, but 'terribly camp'.

Our bedroom was lovely, with gardens outside and sweeping views. In the morning a maid showed us to a dining room where our breakfast was all laid out, and Miss Gillette joined us for coffee. She seemed very pleased to see my mother but told us that she got tired easily, but that Nick would be all ours during the visit and he would be our tour guide. My mother didn't seem very pleased about this and was already restless. It was just like her to want to be somewhere else, even when we had just arrived at the place she had been so keen to get to.

I knew that we had come as much to visit something called the Racquet Club as to see Miss Gillette, but I wasn't sure what it was or why. The Racquet Club had a swimming pool and a Bamboo Room, and must have had something else very special about it, as it was only when my mother had discovered that it was right next door to where Miss Gillette lived, on North Indian Canyon Drive, that she had become determined to make the trip here at all.

'Of course, Clark Gable was a regular at the club, he loved to play tennis there,' my mother told Nick, as if Clark Gable was an old friend of hers that she knew all about. She'd also seen magazine pictures of Marilyn Monroe in her white bikini draped across the club's diving board and Sinatra in the restaurant.

'I understand the Saturday-night dances there are legendary?' she said, as if Nick might go to these. It was clear that she was dying to see this club, and she mentioned it a few times until Miss Gillette said that she would try to arrange for us to have lunch there.

Nick told us, 'Really you have to be a member, and it is very, very exclusive, but of course Miss Gillette knows Frank Bogert!' This was the mayor of Palm Springs, who was very important. He then said proudly, 'Miss Gillette has permitted me to call the mayor's office on your behalf.'

He came back triumphant, having got us a table, and went to change into even smarter clothes. He then drove us around on a tour of the town in the spacious air-conditioned car but my mother checked her little gold watch constantly. At noon we at last drove through the security gate of the Racquet Club and walked across to the pool area where tables were set for lunch. The three of us sat down and ordered our food, but I could see this wasn't enough and my mother had some plan. On a trip to the bathroom I saw her stop to talk to someone and she finally managed to get the manager to come over to our table.

She explained to him, as I had heard her do so many times, 'I'm a newspaper reporter over from England, so I'd love to know a little more about the background of the club so that I can write a double-spread feature for our readers, something that captures the glamour of its history, with some great photos.'

She beamed up at him. 'I'm just so excited to be here myself, after hearing so much about it from Mr Bogert. I was delighted when he arranged this lunch for us, so kind of him.'

The manager became very friendly at the mention of Mr Bogert's name; he fetched a book of photographs and talked about the club and all its famous visitors.

He said that, although the club prided itself on its discretion, he felt able to inform us that right now Paul Newman was having tennis lessons over on the next court and Frank Sinatra had been in for dinner at the weekend. Audrey got him talking about Sinatra, who she said she had met once at Paramount studios. The manager said that Mr Sinatra had been in to check if the caviar was the right colour for a party he was holding there, and how everyone loved him – he was the biggest tipper in town. Sinatra had once dropped a fifty-dollar bill on the floor of the Bamboo Room, and then told them to just leave it there because, he said, 'Think how happy the cleaner will be when he finds it in the morning!'

My mother was very excited by all this. She was looking around a lot, and seemed agitated. I grew to know and understand this state she got into, where she would be distressed by her inability to make the most of an opportunity. She had gained access to this exclusive enclave, but was at a loss to know what to do with it. So what if Sinatra was here days ago, or if Paul Newman was on the next tennis court? She could hardly invite him to join us. Soon our lunch would be over, and we would be back in the confines of Miss Gillette's luxury compound with nothing to show for it. That was the way her mind worked.

She had to think quickly. She asked if there was anyone who the manager thought might agree to a short interview about the club for her newspaper column. This bought her some time and the manager went to talk to a man who was sitting across the restaurant at a far table. The two men glanced over at us, and then the man got up and came over to our table with the manager who introduced him.

'This is Tony Burke, a fellow Englishman. But Mr Burke knows Palm Springs better than most of the Americans who live here.'

Tony still had a London accent with a hint of cockney, although he said that he had lived in the desert resort for over thirty years. He told us that when he felt homesick he played a record he had of the bells at St Margaret's in Westminster mingled with the traffic and noise of London. He could then picture the Embankment on a wet night with the rain reflecting the lights and shadows on its mirror-like surface.

'There are things I miss,' he told us. 'I still have Fortnum's marmalade with my toast in the morning, but just look at all this!' He gestured around. 'The place, the sunshine and palm trees – unbeatable.'

He said that Harry Selfridge, who founded the London department store, had once told him, 'It isn't money you need, but to be where the money is.'

'Best advice anyone ever gave me,' he said. 'Palm Springs has done pretty well for me. In fact I started as a journo like you, with the *LA Times*, then I worked with all the news channels like Pathé on their movie-star news stories. I've mixed with the Hollywood elite and eaten the finest foods . . .'

My mother pretended to scrawl some shorthand in her notebook, but was too fascinated to do much of this. I could see that she really liked him, as she lit up while talking to him. He had an easy charm and a big laugh, and they shared a sense of fun as well as a love of movie gossip.

She drew out all his stories: about the time he took Albert Einstein on a tour of the town; and about the Rodeo where he lent his cowboy hat to Marilyn Monroe. He was a great storyteller,, and I could feel my mother's hopes flickering like the lines on a heart monitor, the signal sometimes weaker, sometimes stronger. I knew how much she wanted some kind of continuation: an offer of dinner, or to visit his home.

But time was up. Nick was doing a polite little cough which I think meant he needed to leave. She finally asked Tony, 'So, do you have any family out here?'

He grinned. 'I'm not the marrying kind.' He got up and shook her hand. 'It was great to meet you ladies; sounds like quite some adventure that you two are on!'

And that was it. Tony Burke wasn't going to sweep us off to a new life in Palm Springs, nor was he going to come back to London and buy a flat for us all where he could hear the bells of Westminster without him needing to play a record.

After Audrey had made one final bathroom trip to peer at Paul Newman through a hedge, we just had to leave with no chance of ever returning or seeing Tony Burke again.

Back at Miss G's, my mother was in her caged-tiger mode, pacing the room as she faced a dull evening; it all brought on a feeling of longing that I knew ate away at her. Nick had made it clear that he took a little time off for himself in the evening, as did the housekeeper, but dinner had been organized for us in the dining room at 6 p.m. At teatime Miss G finally appeared in a long evening dress, and took us out into the garden leaning on Nick's arm as she walked. She led us all to a big orange tree, then pulled down a branch and plucked a fruit, as she explained that when she first came to this house she would squeeze these oranges for breakfast and this tree was her favourite.

Then something very sad had happened, she told us. Someone she was very fond of, extremely fond of, died suddenly, and she said she would show us what transpired beckoning us into the house as she carried the orange with her. Nick obviously knew this story, as he shot past her into the kitchen to prepare a chopping board and knife. We all went in as she held the orange she had picked and rather shakily tried to cut it in half. Nick took over, severed the orange and pulled it apart.

'There!' she said dramatically. 'My orange tree had turned its oranges blood red. How do you explain that?'

My mother, for once, had no answer, and was struggling to be attentive. Miss G then announced that our visit had meant a lot to her and that she wished for us to have something special from the house to remember her by.

Audrey perked up at this latest offering, hoping that perhaps our trip out here had not been in vain. Miss G said that Nick would show us some of the things that she had picked out and we could choose a gift each: something for me and something for Audrey. My mother made an excuse for us to go to our room to wash our hands, where she quickly whispered that when we were shown the possible presents she would nudge me.

This was the signal that I should choose that particular thing. We went back to Miss G and Nick. It was rather like the prizes on a game show, as Nick had laid out the things on a table and he gestured to them theatrically as Miss G described them.

'This is a fine example of the Fabergé style, from the Russian court,' said Miss G, as Nick waved his arms at a pretty decorated oval box like an Easter egg.

'Then these Georgian snuff boxes are delightful, with this delicate enamel decoration.' Nick gave a sort of ballerina wave towards some little boxes.

'Ah! This here might be just the thing for Sally. It's *Grimm's Fairy Tales*, with illustrations by Arthur Rackham. It's a first edition.'

Nick was waving at an old leather book with beautiful pictures in it that I would have loved to have. I had run out of books and was plodding through something I'd found in the house called *The Carpetbaggers*, although I'd failed to work out what a carpetbagger was. It was obvious Miss G wanted me to have this lovely book, but I was still waiting for the nudge.

Then, when we came to an emerald and diamond ring, my mother nudged me gently so I said that it was very nice. Miss G didn't seem sure, and asked if it was the best thing for a young girl, but my mother quickly said it would be perfect for when I was older. She chose a necklace for herself, but when we got back to the room she seemed very pleased with the ring, which I never saw again.

Before we left I asked her once more about when she had met Miss G again, after the time they met on the ship. Miss G had asked my mother about her travels after she had left New York, and had produced a faded postcard, written by Audrey from Antoine's in New Orleans. For once my mother had seemed reluctant to talk about it, biting her lip and changing the subject. Miss G looked at her sadly, but didn't press her.

Now I tried myself, eyeing the box containing my emerald ring. I'd done as I was told, after all.

'Was it fun travelling round America in those days?' I asked, hoping to gently lead her to the story.

'Yes, there used to be a wonderful train from New York called the Super Chief. It was the first sleeping-car train in America, so I spent my prize money on a ticket to Los Angeles; they called it the Train of the Stars because of the number of celebrities who used it. The dining car offered champagne breakfast with Santa Fe French toast.' She sighed at the memory of these past luxuries.

The train had taken her through the farmlands of Kansas and Missouri, the rocky river valleys of Colorado, the deserts of Arizona and New Mexico, before it arrived in California two days later and made a special stop in Pasadena for celebrities to disembark before the crush of LA's Union Station.

By then she was into her story and carried on.

She had found a cheap hotel room and written another letter:

Dear Mr Gable,

I don't know if you will remember our meeting in Southport, when I was lucky enough to give you tea and accompany you on a tour of the town . . .

Then she took a bus to the gates of Paramount studios and hand-delivered it.

The grim hotel she was in, and the sheer size of Los Angeles, almost defeated her. Her money would soon run out, and she felt lonely and overwhelmed. She missed James terribly, but didn't want to go home without a Hollywood story for him, so in a panic she went through her book with its many contacts, the tattered scraps of paper with scribbled names and numbers. She dug out Miss Gillette's elegant gilt-edged card and wrote to the address, suggesting that they might meet for tea.

It wasn't long before a reply came inviting her to stay, and soon afterwards Miss Gillette's chauffeur was whisking her off into the great wide avenues of Beverly Hills and through the gates of Miss G's lavish Italianate villa. Audrey had yet again landed squarely on her little feet, and it was only a few days later that a letter arrived for her, forwarded by the hotel, from the Publicity Department at Paramount:

On behalf of Mr Gable we invite you to visit the studios next week, Tuesday 11th April. We hope that Mr Gable will have an opportunity to greet you in person.

On the appointed day she presented herself at the gate and was taken on a tour of the studio backlot. She saw Dorothy Lamour playing a countess in the set of a Mexican bar, and then waited for some time before a publicist took her to a row of small bungalows buried among gardens of deep foliage. She felt that she was really in Oz now and had finally infiltrated the land of the movie stars. They walked into the one of the bungalows and there was Gable eating a sandwich. The publicist introduced 'Miss Audrey Miller, from England' and he stood to shake her hand.

'You probably don't remember our meeting in Southport. I came quite a way to say hello to you, didn't I?'

He laughed. 'Well, of course I remembered. The Palace Club in England. That is really something!'

She said cheekily, 'Yes, and it was a long, long way from Southport to Melrose Avenue, so I hope I will be getting that return cup of tea.'

He looked at her, impressed, and laughed again.

She was given tea, and he asked her about her adventures so far. He was relishing her story of the radio show when a visitor walked in to see him, a young actor called Rand Brooks who had acted with him in *Gone with the Wind*. Gable introduced them, suggesting to Rand that he show Audrey the town. Rand said that it would be a pleasure and as he left he made a date to meet her.

While Gable took a phone call Audrey stepped out of the bungalow into the warm damp air. It was just starting to rain, the sky was darkening, when Frank Sinatra, holding a drink, stepped out of the nearby bungalow – he put out his hand to catch a raindrop and smiled. They shared a joke, he laughed and raised his glass to her before disappearing back into the shadows.

Audrey practically danced all the way back to Beverly Hills to tell Miss Gillette how she'd had tea with Clark Gable, and actually sat in his very own personal bungalow and he'd called her Honey; she'd talked to Frank Sinatra and made him laugh, and now Rand Brooks was going to take her out for the evening.

She ran up to her room and wrote a long account of her day to James, giving him her new address in Beverly Hills. She imagined him being so pleased and impressed by all she had done. A couple of nights later she was writing another letter describing how Rand had taken her to Santa Monica where there was dancing on the pier, and the moon shone on the ocean. A group called the Make Believes were performing, and one of them knew Rand, and they all ended up drinking beer together.

The entertainers were good company; their affectionate banter made her laugh. They were looking for someone to help out on their tour, taking tickets and booking things, and she told them that she might be interested. It seemed almost churlish to turn her back on these chances, she told herself, and she knew that James would agree. After all, it would only be for a few weeks.

Miss G did sound a note of caution. There was a way she had, of simply raising one of her eyebrows, that Audrey sometimes found hard to decipher, but Audrey was quick to reassure her hostess that James had wanted her to have a big

Mum at Antoine's, New Orleans, with a friend.

adventure before they settled down. Just a week or two later Audrey was off on the road with a promise to Miss G to send her a picture from Antoine's.

'So you sent it?' I asked.

'Yes,' she replied, but didn't look at me.

'Did you eat snails?'

She nodded with a look of misery.

She was now anxious that we should be on our way, and became more cheerful again as she pushed Tony Burke's card into the book of contacts and pulled out a new one. It was for a ship's purser called Dick.

12

Sally and Audrey at Sea

ONCE THE SUITCASES were back out on the bed, my mother was happy again and any disappointments were forgotten. I was excited that now we could go on a ship, the ship that Dick worked on as a purser. A cruise sounded moonlit and romantic, and as we packed she talked about the 'rituals', which sounded like something that painted warriors did, whooping and dancing around a fire.

These rituals were, she said, the 'Neptune crossing', a fancy-dress party and a Hawaiian luau. I asked what we would wear to a fancy-dress party, and she started to create characters out of our suitcase clothes; she pulled out her black catsuit and my black trousers and said we could make little ears and tails and sing 'What's New Pussycat?' and she sang about my pussycat eyes, making big eyes and stroking her invisible whiskers, and my pussycat nose, kissing my nose. I learnt the words and we sang it together. I knew that the faster I grew up, the more she loved me and the more we were a team.

Then she grabbed her leopard-print bikini and wrap and said, 'Or the Flintstones?' We tried them on – I pulled up her underslip to my armpits like a dress – and sang the 'Yabba Dabba Doo' song, me as usual rather tunelessly, and did a Flintstones duet. I watched us in the mirrors and thought we looked great.

I had high hopes that the cruise ship was exactly what we'd been looking for: full of love possibilities for her, and places for me to explore. We were sailing from Miami, but we arrived there with hardly any time to look around. My mother wanted to visit a huge hotel called the Fontainebleau where they had filmed a James Bond film, so we stopped there for coffee and, when she noticed an old actor called Cesar Romero in the lobby, she spent so long talking to him that we had to run to get our bags to board the ship.

Walking up to the ship was even better than we'd hoped, with the calm, blue ocean and promise of the horizon ahead of us. At the top of the gangway stood the crew in crisp white uniforms waiting to greet us, and at the bottom was a gaggle of photographers ready to take our picture. My mother had a new dress with a pretty sun hat and matching raffia clutch bag, and spent ages posing for them and making them laugh, but I wanted her to hurry as I couldn't wait to see our cosy cabin. I loved the idea that this huge hotel on the water would float right up to all these exotic ports and our little cabin would float there with us.

The next day I woke dying to explore, but found, to my horror, that I was being sent to something called the Little Neptune Club where a hatchet faced woman called

Miss Hicks forced us children to play board games and do jigsaw puzzles. My mother hoped that I would make friends there, but there was no one my age, and I just desperately wanted to roam about the ship trying to get into places where I wasn't allowed. There were bars, a casino, engine rooms, the pool and cinema to see. Instead I was sitting playing Beetle under the eagle eye of Miss Hicks, fizzing with frustration.

In the evening we shared big tables in the restaurant with other passengers and here I would hear my mother's stories and the gasps and laughter that greeted them. I was aware that she had a couple of what she told me were 'possibilities' and I knew she meant for love. One was Dick, the purser, but quite soon into our trip she told another lady that she had realized that he was a 'confirmed bachelor, if you know what I mean, nudge, nudge, wink, wink'.

The person she seemed to really like was a man called Roger, but he was married. He was the husband of a lady called Jet, who had a lot of colourful eye-catching outfits that my mother commented on; but Roger didn't seem to get on with his wife at all. No one seemed to like Jet as she wasn't very kind to Roger and she often got drunk. Roger seemed to like my mother a lot, and she was different around him: kinder and quieter. One night Jet got drunk and did a mean impersonation of Roger with a man who had once been rude to them at a petrol station. She thought she was being funny but no one was laughing. My mother had been trying to talk to Roger and ignore Jet, but then suddenly she turned and said, 'Do you think you might have been a little bit squiffy at the time, Jet? Perhaps you started the quarrel and Roger was just trying to defend you?' Everyone stared at Audrey and then started talking about something else loudly, but Jet really didn't like my mother after that and wouldn't sit at a table with her again. That made it hard for my mother to talk to Roger any more, but she sometimes wandered about and I knew she was looking for him, hoping that he would be on his own.

I did make friends on the cruise. One was Humphrey, an old man who was an actor, and although he looked frail he had a proper actor kind of voice, deep and booming. We met when he noticed me reading, and told me that he sat up on deck most afternoons after lunch. He offered to find me some books that I might enjoy and said he hoped we could have some more chats. Something about his kind smile reminded me of Mr Naylor, the manager at Marshall's in Southport, and I liked him a lot.

We had sailed from Miami with our odd assortment of passengers. There were very few families and a lot of couples, a fact that my mother constantly mentioned.

Humphrey came to find me a day or two later with some books he had got for me in the ship's library. He said he would show me where it was, and I should read some classics of both children's and adult literature as I had the vivid imagination of a child, but the conversation of an adult. I loved *The Secret Garden* and *Peter Pan*, but also was intrigued by *The Mill on the Floss* and Pip's adventures in *Great Expectations*. Pip's love for Miss Havisham's Estella reminded me of the strange cruelty that Philip seemed to almost enjoy in

Of Human Bondage, as if people loved even more those who were unkind to them.

I mentioned to Humphrey about my own novel. I had begun a story about a model, Natasha, and her photographer Jason who are destined to fall in love but are continually thwarted by events and other suitors. It was called *Around the World with an Air of Romance*. I was pleased with the title and my idea for the story, but secretly afraid that my missing school was going to mean that I'd be no good as a writer. When Humphrey presented me with a notebook and suggested that I note things down in it – details of people and places that might one day be useful in my writing – it felt like a sign. Simply by calling me a writer he made me feel encouraged. He said everything that happened to you, good and bad, was material for your books, and this was a good way to survive things, as you didn't mind so much if you could turn them into stories. This made me wonder about my mother, and how much of what we did was 'material' for her stories and whether it helped her to survive things.

I was still being sent down daily to Miss Hicks's club, which my mother saw as her babysitter and ticket to freedom. I pleaded to be released and finally pretended to go but instead ran off to explore on my own.

The ship was an extraordinary floating world. In my notebook I wrote down descriptions and things that happened, thinking these might be material for what Natasha and Jason did on board. There were lots of bars and lounges and three restaurants of varying levels of grandeur. My mother was working in the middle one, as a hostess showing people to their tables. It had a buffet heaped with foods from different countries. The grandest one was quieter, the tables set further apart and covered with thick white tablecloths. There was a ballroom with a stage and nightly entertainments.

One day the cinema was screening a Disney comedy called *That Darned Cat* and I went along after lunch and saw a pretty ponytailed girl walking in with her mother and another girl who looked a bit younger. I was sitting on my own, and the mother came over and said hello.

'This is Peter and Maxine,' she said. 'Why don't you all sit together?'

The older girl, Peter, was American and gave me a 'three is a crowd' look, but Maxine was the same age as me, English, and friendly. She had red hair and freckles, and told me helpfully that Peter had a boy's name because she was American.

The lights went down and *That Darned Cat* began as the ship rolled on towards Fiji. The film was made even funnier by Maxine's helpless giggles. Maxine wanted to turn everything into a joke, which shattered any remaining ice between us. Peter and I became completely infected by her hysteria. We didn't know if we were giggling at the film or at the pink helpless heap that was Maxine, but we all wept with laughter until we couldn't breathe and our tummies hurt.

After that the three of us became inseparable. Luckily my mother decided that if I was in the company of other girls, and one was older, no harm would come to me and I was free from the horrors of Miss Hicks.

Inspired by mystery and adventure novels, which Peter and I both loved, we agreed that we three should form a gang and start looking out for adventures on board.

Maxine had another interest, similar to my own, which was 'Lovers', and we began to think of ways these ideas could come together . . . Adventures and Lovers. She had a young Irish nanny back in London who she adored, and who discussed her love affairs at length with Maxine, who now knew about French kissing, which was put in the mix with Peter's information about WHT or 'wandering hand trouble', which boys had when you got older.

I was able to contribute quite a bit more technical information, as my mother had already given me some useful tips that were unusual to pass on to a girl of nine: for example that I had a magic button down below in my pussycat. Peter and Maxine received this news solemnly and didn't mention whether or not they had found their own magic buttons yet. Between us we had a fair idea of what went on with sex. Peter regarded it with cool interest and was already conscious of her growing power over boys. Maxine of course discussed it with feverish hilarity, and I had my personal reasons for wanting to understand its complexities and how it was shaping my and my mother's lives.

They were interested in my writing, and Maxine had the idea of using the trip for some useful research into 'Lovers' for my novel. There were many on board – some honeymooners, and some having wedding anniversaries – although we decided that this latter category were too old to be lovers, so should be ignored.

We took to stalking couples, and found the best time of all was on deck in the early evening with a beautiful sunset turning the sky and the water rose pink and violet. Everywhere lovers stood in pairs, leaning against the rails and gazing in rapture at the view and at each other. We saw Roger and Jet taking an evening stroll; they stopped and both looked unhappily out to sea. I had told the girls all about Roger and Jet, and pointed them out in the dining room. Maxine was now quite fascinated and kept staring at him, which was embarrassing.

Peter was very disapproving of my mother's interest in Roger and said that if he and my mother became lovers it would be something called an affair, and he would have to get a divorce and everyone would hate him. I wrote this down in my notebook, and wondered if my character Jason might have a drunk wife back home and be having an 'affair' with Natasha. Peter's parents knew someone who did all that and nobody talked to him any more. When she told me this, I privately thought that it wouldn't matter, as people didn't talk to my mother in Southport anyway, and at least she would have Roger.

One night my mother and Roger sat alone in the dining room after everyone had left. Jet had gone to bed, as my mother said, 'a little the worse for wear', which meant drunk. I sat with my book, looking engrossed as they talked in low voices. My mother was telling Roger about her youthful adventures, and had got to the story of 'The Three Make Believes'. There were sometimes two versions of her tales – a happy one and a sadder one – but I could tell by her voice that this tale she was recounting to Roger was a very truthful one, so I listened with care.

The story she told to Roger began with the Make Believes and her rattling off down the highway from LA in an old school bus, which the three musicians had adapted to take them across the country.

They drove for thousands of miles, through Utah and Colorado, past cliffs of red rock and through endless sandstone desert, through pine-covered mountains with snowy peaks and mountain towns that looked like the Wild West.

They saw jazz on Basin Street in New Orleans and watched a funeral go by, and yes, she did get to the legendary Antoine's restaurant that Louis Jourdan had told her about that night in New York, and she'd dined on oysters and snails.

They finally set off on the trip back to New York, which took them through North Carolina. As they drove across the scrubby barren landscape towards the coast, the bus navigated its way along back roads and over rickety wooden bridges to the sliver-thin barrier islands known as the Outer Banks. Nag's Head was then an even tinier beach town, perched at the tip of the northernmost island between Kitty Hawk and the Kill Devil Hills.

The casino had been the great hangout for servicemen during the war, and was famous for having the best dance floor on the coast and a no-shoes policy. Everyone threw off their footwear at the bottom of the narrow wooden stairway before climbing to the second floor where the wooden boards gleamed in the lamplight. The owner's secret to his legendary

Mum (right) at the beach, USA, 1946.

dance floor was bowling-alley wax, so the barefoot dancers slid and slithered across it as they jived, only pausing to take a breath by the broad windows that were propped open to let in the sea breeze. Each night the cool salty air wafted in and the music and laughter wafted out onto the beach below.

That night Audrey had danced for hours, until the sun was coming up and they all ran laughing into the sea to rinse the sweat from their exhausted bodies. She was suddenly caught in the moment – the sky washed in pink, the distant shrieking of her friends along the beach, the sea foaming at her ankles – and had a fleeting sense of intense happiness.

The image of James smiling down at her with his steady gaze made her feel almost weak with longing, and she couldn't wait to go home.

Only a week or two later Audrey was looking dreamily out of the window of the bus that finally carried them all into New York. As it drove through suburbs of leafy streets, she watched mothers with babies, families meeting children off the school bus, and imagined herself in a house with James and their children playing happily in the back garden. She hugged herself with anticipation at the thought of arriving home and rushing into his arms. It had been months rather than weeks, and she had so much to tell him.

She was finally dropped off and made her way back to Sadie's apartment in Jackson Heights. Her godmother greeted her with a big hug, but her face was grim and Audrey knew immediately that something was wrong. Sadie handed her the stack of envelopes: letters from her mother, from Jean and from James. Some had been forwarded by Miss Gillette's secretary to New Orleans, where a landlady had then forwarded them on up to New York. The letters looked battered and exhausted from their long journey and were now grubby with stamps and forwarding labels as she tore them open.

She began with the earliest date and her mother's first letters telling her how loyal James had been in coming to visit her, bringing her flowers, and looking lovingly through her albums of pictures of Audrey.

The letters from James told a similar story. The early ones were sweet, eager and loving, and full of interest at her amazing adventures. But the later ones sounded hurt and concerned, and he asked her repeatedly for a return date. The last one said that, as she hadn't responded with a date, he was now assuming that her feelings for him had changed.

Rebecca's letters then delivered the alarming news that Janet, a girl who had been evacuated from Coventry and stayed on in Southport, was spending more time with him. James had begun playing tennis with Janet most days, and meeting up with their friends at the pub on summer evenings.

Audrey sat, white-faced and uncomprehending, as Sadie then read out her own letter from Rebecca.

I can hardly bear to think how my darling will feel, but James and Janet announced their engagement last Saturday. He had been round to see me and told me that his last letter to Audrey had never had a reply. I asked him to please wait, but he said his mind was made up, and that all his friends and family agreed that it was all for the best. He said that he and Janet wanted the same things: children and a quiet family life. They didn't see any reason for a long engagement and were arranging the wedding for that same summer.

Audrey took the next berth she could get on the *Queen Mary* home. It was a very different journey from the one she had taken a few months before and she spent those days in silent shock. She then caught the first train she could from

Southampton up to Southport. Her mother tried to stop her, but she just left her bags and went straight to James's parents' house.

James's father opened the door and called for James, who appeared, looking defensive. They left the house and walked together through the pinewoods along the beach near his home. She wept, pleaded, apologized, made excuses, pleaded again. He was cold and withdrawn. She tried to put her arms around him, to bury her face in his neck and smell that familiar smell.

'Don't,' he said angrily.

She felt as though something in him had broken.

'I'd believed that there was this strong thread between us,' she told Roger that night on the cruise ship, as I eavesdropped. 'It was stronger than thousands of miles, or an ocean; it would have gone around the world several times and not snapped. I felt it, I felt it all the time I was away, every moment of every day.'

But James didn't believe this, and he was so different that she hardly recognized him. He told her, 'It was only after a month or two that I realized you never even talked about wanting children or running a home. All those letters from America were about meeting "fascinating people" and seeing the world. You seemed to be always chasing some dream, and I realized that you always would be.'

He began to walk back towards his house very fast. In her skirt and heels she couldn't match his long strides and as she called after him her voice was soon lost in the wind whistling through the pines.

Their break-up was something that she believed was her lifelong wound – and it would never fully heal. This was the account she now quietly told to Roger, and it explained so much of what happened later.

When I finally asked her, some years after this, what was her third wish, she looked at me quizzically.

'On the *Queen for a Day* recording, remember they gave you three wishes.'

'Oh,' she said wistfully. 'I said that I wished to go home to my handsome prince, my fiancé, and live happily ever after.'

I then asked her why she had cried at the Nag's Head Casino, and after a moment she said, 'I suppose because that was the last time I was truly happy.'

At last the missing pieces were beginning to fit together. There were gaps, a time that I had heard her describe as her 'London years', but nothing that explained what was for me the most interesting part of the story, which was how I came to be born.

13

I Yabba Dabba Doo!

ONE OF THE MAJOR EVENTS of the cruise's crossing was the fancy-dress gala, and I was secretly hoping that my mother and I would be the best costumes. I knew this would cheer her up and give Roger a chance to see her shine. My actor friend, Humphrey, was going as 'Prospero' from a Shakespeare play, and gave me a book of Shakespeare's stories written for children. He said that if I could tell him who Prospero was by the night of the fancy-dress gala he would make me a gift of the shell necklace which I kept looking at in the shop. I found the character in *The Tempest*, read the story, and won my necklace. He told me that he had once played Prospero, and that the costume only required the rags of a shipwreck survivor, a tall staff and a cape, which suggests magic and sorcery.

He had brought a bedsheet, which we took down to the games room and spread on the floor. Maxine and Peter helped me, and we decorated it with felt pens, drawing moons, stars and magical symbols copied from Humphrey's book, to create a sorcerer's cape for him to wrap around himself.

As we finished the cape Humphrey circled us, saying in his marvellous booming voice:

'The cloud-capped towers, the gorgeous palaces,
The solemn temples, the great globe itself –
Yea, all which it inherit – shall dissolve.
And like this insubstantial pageant faded,
Leave not a rack behind.'

We all sat and looked at him, mesmerized.

Later that evening, we were gathered at a big round table with Humphrey, my mother, Maxine and Peter's parents, and another couple.

The lady asked me if I liked fancy-dress parties and I said, 'I've only been to one. It was on ice. I was wearing a bowler hat and carrying my school recorder and Mummy just pushed me out onto the ice and I didn't know who I was supposed to be.'

My mother interrupted, 'She was Acker Bilk, the jazz musician,' and then turned to me. 'You remember, I told you that you were Acker Bilk.'

'Yes, but I didn't know who Acker Bilk was. And I didn't know how to ice-skate. So for the rest of the party I stood holding onto the side of the rink while the other children came up and asked me who Acker Bill was and when I said, "I don't know," they laughed at me.'

The people at the table seemed to be listening, so I went on.

'Then, one day, a funny thing happened. We were in an

airport and my mum pointed to a man sitting in the waiting area and said, "There's Acker Bilk! Go and get his autograph for me."

'I went and asked him, and while he was writing "To Audrey" I said to him, "I once went to a fancy-dress party as you. Though I didn't know who you were."

'He said, "Well, you know now . . ."'

'I said, "Yes, you play the recorder and ice-skate in a bowler hat."'

Everyone laughed at that, and I thought for a moment that maybe I could tell stories like my mother rather than always sitting at her side not speaking.

It was now the shortlist for the fancy-dress contest. Everyone was to walk across the ballroom stage and announce who we were.

My mother was beckoning me. We had to dance across singing 'We're the Flintstones', and then at the end jump in the air and shout, 'Yabba Dabba Doo!'

I was wearing her leopard-skin half-slip, and she had back-combed my hair into a strange frizz. She looked beautiful in her ocelot silk wrap with a necklace of chicken bones round her neck. We had had to eat chicken all week to get these and then find something called florist wire, which meant I had to dismantle old flower arrangements that we stole from the restaurant tables. She told me that if anyone asked I could say I wanted to decorate our cabin as a surprise for my mummy. So at every meal I carried back the flower arrangements and unwound the wire from them, which she magically turned into chicken-bone jewellery.

We now did our song and dance and she said into the microphone, 'Hey, what did Wilma Flintstone say at the altar when she married Fred?' Then we jumped and both yelled out, 'I Yabba Dabba Doo!' just as we had practised. Everyone gave us a big clap and we got a few cheers. Roger stood up and shouted, 'Bravo!' and my mother did a funny curtsey just for him.

When it was Humphrey's turn, the compère said, 'And now we have the legendary actor Humphrey Leighton revisiting his performance as Prospero.' Humphrey gave some of his 'We are such stuff as dreams are made on' speech. He had practised this and when I said I thought it was 'made of' he showed me and explained it was in Elizabethan. He did it very well, and to our surprise he got a standing ovation. As he wove his way back to our table through the still-clapping guests, I said, 'I didn't know you were famous.' He made a gesture that meant 'thank you' and 'I'm not really so famous' at the same time.

On each voyage there was a Neptune's Crossing ritual held on the day that the ship crossed the equator, and Dick, the purser, was to be the victim being judged by Neptune's court. He always greeted me in a friendly way and I was now rather fond of him and curious to see his trial and sentencing.

He seemed very out of sorts, though, explaining to us girls that he shouldn't be doing it at all.

'I've done the whole damned thing before, pardon my French. So, you see, I'm technically a shellback.'

We nodded sympathetically.

'And it's supposed to be done to an uninitiated non-shellback. It was the Director of Entertainment's turn. But now he's saying that he's coming down with something.'

He looked very gloomy about this.

'So of course, muggins had to step in.'

He meant that he was muggins and not very happy about it.

We had all gathered around the pool, the entire population of our floating island, all shuffling about in sweltering heat on the rather small and cramped deck. Some people were wearing swimming costumes and the air was thick with the smell of suntan lotion, chlorine, ladies' perfume and something else not very nice. Someone announced the arrival of King Neptune, who appeared carrying a trident and wearing a silly hat. Then the victim emerged in his swimming trunks. Maxine said that she was sure my mother wouldn't love the poor purser after seeing this, as his tummy stuck out and his hair stood on end as they broke an egg in it and rubbed it about. Then people threw pies and tomatoes at him, covered him in shaving foam and threw him into the swimming pool as everyone cheered. I felt sorry for him, particularly when I saw my mother trying to stand near Roger and not really watching the ritual at all.

The cruise also made stopovers, and Audrey and I had both been excited by the sound of Tahiti, because there was a native feast, which the purser said was a highlight.

I soon agreed with him about the feast being a highlight. It was almost dark in the vast thatched hut that the coach brought us to that night, except for rows of flaming torches, which lit the strange faces of the wooden Tiki statues.

Mum, Tahiti, 1965.

The men who did the floor show were all shiny with hardly any clothes on and the women wore grass skirts with spikes sticking out around them like huge hedgehogs and swung their hips as if they had no bones and were made of jelly. Roger and Jet were at the feast; when Roger went over to look at the traditional *ahima'a* my mother quickly followed him. The *ahima'a* was a big pit in the ground with hot stones that cooked the food, which was wrapped in banana leaves. I watched as she and Roger talked quietly as if they were saying something important but I couldn't guess what it was.

The next day my mother was subdued and distracted. She

was usually against buying what she called tourist tat even if it was something completely beautiful. She was especially against anything that took up any room in our luggage, so I was amazed when I was allowed to buy one of the straw Hula skirts I'd been longing for. It had the dry grassy smell of the South Seas and I loved it even though I then had to lug it around in a separate carrier bag whenever we moved on.

The native feast was a memorable evening in many ways, as what followed was so unhappy. Roger and Jet got off the cruise at the next stop, to fly home to England, and Roger left a letter for my mother. When she was out of the cabin I found it and read it to see what had made her cry so much. But it said a lot of really kind things: she was 'a very special lady' and had given him 'some super memories that would help with the difficulties that may lie ahead'. He said that he wasn't someone who could walk away from his responsibilities but he hoped that she would find someone who could give her the happiness she deserved. These nice thoughts didn't cheer her up at all, though, and she looked pale and sad in a way I hadn't seen before.

I was talking to Humphrey the next day when we saw her standing on deck gazing out to sea. He sighed and said, 'Ah, Divine Discontent!'

I said that I thought she just wanted to find love, and he said, 'If we truly want to find love, my dear, we see that it is never really very far away from us.'

This didn't seem very fair, as Roger had been married to someone else, and there was no one else nearby. On the other hand it added to my sense that going to all these places was a bit nutty, and I wondered whether there might have been someone perfectly nice closer to home.

A few days after this, we were sitting with a friendly couple who were at our table for dinner. They talked a lot about their son who was a doctor and their home in Tunbridge Wells and house in France. They were kind to my mother and asked her lots of questions. We were by an open window where there was a breeze, and the lady said she wished she'd brought her wrap. Her husband jumped up to go to the cabin and get it; she told him he didn't need to, but then he went anyway. When he came back he put it around her shoulders and poured her a cup of hot coffee. My mother suddenly said she didn't feel well and ran back to our cabin. I followed her and she didn't even go in the door. She leant against the corridor wall outside the cabin, crying and doing a weird shaking thing.

I got her into the cabin at last and tried to cuddle up to her and asked her what was wrong.

She said, 'Why does she get a lovely husband taking care of her and pouring her coffee when she's nothing special?'

It was a question that baffled me: why no one seemed to fall in love with her when she was so beautiful and entertaining and everyone loved hearing her stories and watching her dance. I had got better at cheering her up, so at last she stopped shaking and we snuggled up together on her bed. She squeezed me hard and said, 'Anyway, I have my little precious,' and fell asleep in all her clothes, her face still stained with tears.

The awful thing was that we were doing the whole voyage

all over again as she had signed a contract to work in the dining room, showing people to tables. We were saying our goodbyes and everyone else was disembarking the ship to go home. It was the first time she seemed really worried that I might be bored. She hugged me, and said, as she sometimes would, 'I'm sorry, I shouldn't be dragging you around like this. But we have some fun, don't we?' She promised that we would go to New Zealand and see the cousins I wanted to see. My father had a brother who had gone to live in New Zealand and had two boys who I had never met. She had been thinking of skipping this and I had begged her not to.

The second voyage of the cruise seemed to go on for ever. The fact that I'd had real friends on the first voyage now gave me a desolate feeling that I could now name as loneliness on these later crossings. The corridors all reminded me of dashing about exploring with Maxine and Peter. The cinema was where we had all spent that first afternoon in helpless giggles over *That Darned Cat*.

My mother and I completed the circuit of the cruise more than once, but I'm not sure if we did the whole journey two or three times. After that first one the fancy-dress balls were dull; we always went as the Flintstones, and our shout of 'Yabba Dabba Doo!' fell flat, and just made me remember Humphrey in his lovely cloak. The ship felt smaller and smaller and the feeling of panic I'd had in the Kill Devil Hills began to come back.

My mother was in a terrible mood, and sometimes lay on her bed for no reason, just staring at the ceiling. We always collected terrible jokes to tell each other, as she had once said, 'Even bad jokes can be funny if you tell them right,' so we would come up with awful ones to test out her theory.

'Why did the sea monster eat six ships full of potatoes?'

She shook her head. 'I don't know.'

'Cos nobody can eat just one potato ship!'

But all I got from her now was the faintest smile. She began asking me all the time if I was all right and at last pulled herself together to at least sing songs with me. Our favourite was 'We're a Couple of Swells', which we did with our arms around each other and a skipping dance that we performed along the corridor on the way to dinner and we would laugh when people came out of their cabins and saw us.

It was a great relief when she finally told me that we were going to disembark for good at the New Zealand stopover to see my cousins and then go on to Australia. I loved the very word 'cousin', and would repeat it in my head. I overheard a lady, who my mother had tried not very successfully to befriend, telling her husband that Audrey and 'that poor child' were getting off because the cruise was 'clearly not the happy hunting ground she hoped it would be'.

It was only some months later that my mother showed me a newspaper page with a large picture of Humphrey and a headline that said ACTOR HUMPHREY LEIGHTON HAS DIED. 'That's your nice actor friend, what a shame,' she sighed. He had given me the book of Shakespeare stories and written in it with his spidery scrawl: 'To Sally from her friend Humphrey. Live the creative life, my dear. It is full of wonders.'

14

The Antipodes

I LOVED MY COUSIN, Stew, devotedly from the moment we met. He was standing with his brother D'Arcy and his parents – my father's brother, Donald, and his wife Glynis – waiting to meet us as we disembarked from the ship. My mother waved when she saw them, and I skipped beside her in excitement, for here were my longed-for cousins. D'Arcy was blond and handsome, Stew darker and sturdier; neither had much to say to me but I hoped that their approval could be won. Perhaps I could show them our Flintstones routine or we could all watch *That Darned Cat* together.

We drove to their beautiful house in Auckland, right on a big white sandy beach with the surf rolling just beyond their deck where we had a barbecue. My mother said it was a ranch-style house, and had told people that Takapuna Beach was the best place to live and that Glynis and Donald had done very well for themselves. Glynis was now an actress in a soap opera and Donald was in insurance. I heard her tell someone that she hoped they might help her, but I didn't know in what way.

My mother didn't feel we could stay very long, which was disappointing as New Zealand was a place of marvels. It had hot springs and Maoris, as well as my cousins. Stew was very boyish and rather ingeniously building a rocket in their basement. He allowed me to help, and I found it completely absorbing in a way that girly activities rarely seemed to be. Girls usually chattered, which was enjoyable but distracting. Boys, it seemed, liked to work without talking and it made for a different kind of friendship, one that felt deeper because it was unspoken but built on a shared vision. Stew struck me as almost a genius. His rocket was huge and seemed perfectly convincing. We could both get inside it and view the control panels. He would give me a task, like painting the cardboard bits silver, and then we would both work away in contented silence. He seemed to approve of me and said that one day, if he wasn't too busy as an astronaut, he might have a farm that I could come and help on where we could have cows and horses and a tractor. This was to become my idea of a perfect future: that one day Stew and I could have a farm together. We would work alongside each other all day, feeding the animals, planting seeds and watching them grow through the summer, till autumn came and we harvested our abundant crops.

The visit was painfully short. It seemed cruel that we had been in so many places where I had absolutely nothing to do, and now when I was busy and completely happy, we were already having to leave. I cried on the plane, but at least I had a dream now. After we left New Zealand this became a happy game of mine – farming with Stew – and the fantasy lingered in my imagination for years. His was the opposite to the jittery distracted energy of my mother; he was calm and quietly devoted to a task with a clear end goal. He explained exactly what we needed to do and why. It made me look forward to the idea of one day having a purpose, a structure to my life – a job.

Afterwards I would daydream, staring out of windows, as I busily imagined the daily routines and walked us through them. At 6 a.m. we had our breakfast and put on boots to go and milk the cows . . . and so on till bedtime. It gave a shape to the day that I loved. Or I would find things in our hotel room – belts and rolled-up towels – to mark out fields and farm buildings on a carpet and play make believe as I moved my Barbie and Ken dolls in between these spaces, acting out the daily jobs that Stew and I undertook. I felt a deep satisfaction at the thought of filling a pail with water for a thirsty cow, or pouring grain into its feeding trough. I had never before understood or fully grasped the concept of play, something that made friendships with other children tricky. But now I did.

The agony of leaving made the next stop feel even more pointless. Sydney was supposed to be hot, but it rained non-stop. My mother had a secret mission of some kind, and it required her to be alone. She noticed that the cinema right by our hotel was showing *The Sound of Music* and told me that I would like it. So she bought my ticket and then left me there with a key for our room, pointing out how close the two places were and making me promise not to go anywhere else. I had instructions to go back to the hotel once the film finished, and order from room service if I was hungry. Then I should read or watch TV till she returned.

The cinema was cosy after the wet streets, and families rustled and ate popcorn in the darkness. Then the big red curtain went up, and Maria raced across the mountaintop, swirled her arms around herself in rapture and burst into full-throated song: 'The hills are alive . . .'

I seemed to dissolve into the screen and into her. It was one of those sublime childhood moments when you find something perfect, and life suddenly makes sense. I was Maria and right there in the Austrian Alps with a wonky nun haircut and apron. I was a flibbertigibbet, a will-o'-the-wisp, a clown. I was making the Von Trapp children clothes out of the curtains. I was cycling through the countryside and falling in love with their father. When the film finished, as the family walked off across the mountains to freedom, I realized that there was another showing, and waited for it to start all over again.

After the two shows I was hungry and worried my mother would be back and looking for me, so rushed straight to the hotel room. It was empty so I practised being Maria, rushing around the room, jumping on the bed and singing as loudly as I could into the fresh mountain air. I was exhilarated and in love with life.

It was quite late when my mother eventually appeared, and it seemed that the mission had not been accomplished. She looked relieved when I suggested that if she was busy I would like to see the film again. The rain continued all week and I spent my time rushing between the cinema to watch two successive shows and then practice sessions in our hotel with room-service sandwiches as fuel for the energetic dance moves. I now knew the film by heart.

I was suddenly busy. After playing 'Being Maria' I could make a farm and play my game, happily running through the work routine that Stew and I would follow. I'd also had the brilliant idea of finishing my novel this way – with Natasha telling Jason to go back to his wife, and then marrying a kind farmer she'd met in New Zealand, and working alongside him all day in dungarees, tending their crops and animals.

I was even sorry when Audrey said that we were leaving, as I was so taken up with the film and the novel, but she promised me that *The Sound of Music* would be on in a lot of places all over the world. The suitcases were on the bed now anyway, and there was little I could do. 'Where are we going?' I'd ask. There was the jokiness that wasn't even funny. She'd say somewhere that sounded far away like 'Timbuctu!' 'What country is it in?' 'Neverland.' 'No but really Mummy?'

Penang sounded real at least. Where was it? What had she been doing? Had something happened to make her suddenly decide that we were off again?

'Three questions.' Penang was 'in Malaysia, it had beaches'. I asked her what she had been doing, but she ignored me. I tried asking if she had done anything interesting, and she finally relented and said that she'd had one fun expedition and had wished I was there. She was with someone who was a famous inventor, and they had been in a car that travelled on the water.

'It was very odd when it drove off the edge of the harbour and splashed down into the sea,' she told me, 'but was great fun once you got going and drove it through the water.' I wondered who on earth this man was, and if he was about to enter our story.

It seemed that he wasn't and was never mentioned again. The intriguing anecdote was all I would get, and was part of a mysterious life that she appeared to sometimes be leading when she was away from me: one that would only be revealed in odd jigsaw pieces that didn't fit in anywhere at all. This piece had apparently been discarded now, and a couple of days later our show was 'back on the road'.

By the time we had boarded our plane she had already found a new friend. The lady who was sitting next to us seemed to like her a lot, and they soon fell into conversation. After a while the woman, who was perhaps a bit older than my mother, became upset – something about her son that had saddened her – and then I could see it coming; I dreaded these moments. One of my mother's worst traits was giving firm and persuasive advice to complete strangers; it never sounded quite right to me when her own life was so completely off the tracks, and I wanted to shout 'Stop!'

The woman she was now talking to had taken out a pad of paper and, perhaps in exchange for some life-changing advice, was writing down an address in Penang. Audrey folded and popped the note in her bag, which was already a bottomless repository for such scraps.

Occasionally, when it seemed we had come to a particularly difficult fork on our mysterious road, and there was a question of where, what, when, how, my mother would rummage through her bag, randomly pulling out these bits of paper like some odd party game to determine our next move, frowning at them: 'Now who was Bertrand? Was it that nice man with the moustache who stopped his car and gave us a lift when we got lost somewhere near the Pyramids? . . . rather handsome'; 'Oh, Luxembourg . . . where *is* Luxembourg? It sounds like it's near France?', and so on. I had learnt to dread them, but also to feel the thrill of a lurch into the unknown.

She was very pleased with this latest scrap. 'She's invited us to her club, the Penang blah blah blah,' she said, as if a job was well done, her eyes bright with hope. 'She knows quite a few people out there, I think.' I remember the view from the window of the plane, of an island with silver ribbons of water around it, and my mother saying excitedly, 'Pearl of the Orient.' By now I had learnt to detect in her voice that note of both hope and despondency, as if she already half expected to be let down. I imagined the next time we would be looking down at this island from a plane; it would be when we were leaving and we usually left places with that sense of disappointment, but buoyant in our hope that in the next place things would be better and we *would* really strike lucky. Pearl of the Orient? Her middle name was Pearl, and her most worn piece of jewellery was the rope of pearls that one of her 'fiancés' had given her on their engagement. The pearls had an unusual arrangement, and women would ask about them with interest. She loved that. She would say, 'Yes, they were given to me by a fiancé. Sweet Perry; he was a member of the Guinness family – yes, *that* Guinness – but in the end . . . well . . . it just wasn't the real thing.'

She would pause with that cheeky smile and raised eyebrow. 'Though luckily the pearls are!'

It was another story that I wanted to know more about. Who was Perry, and why wasn't he the real thing?

The lady and my mother were chatting happily when a tremendous jolt shook the plane, followed by another loud crunch and then terrible confusion. People were wailing, children and babies were crying. My mother was shaking, holding my hand too tight. Out of the window a band of furious flames was racing across the wing with roaring engine noise. It was so frightening I could hardly believe it was happening.

Mass panic now rippled through the plane, with passengers shouting to the stewardesses, those lovely BOAC ladies, who somehow managed to calm everyone down. My mother wasn't calming down, her whole body was trembling and I found myself comforting her, saying, 'It will be all right, Mummy.'

'What if it isn't?' she whispered. 'This can't be it!'

Our whole life was built around an idea of 'this can't be it' and a perpetual sense of something incredible waiting for us just around the next bend; so to have never reached Oz, and to die now, hurtling through this blue sky down into the canopy of jungle below, was unthinkable.

We felt ourselves losing height and the captain announced in an unflappable it's-completely-routine voice that we had suffered a malfunction and would be making an emergency landing. The crew reassured us that we were now flying over Borneo, a runway was ready for us and we would be landing there shortly.

My mother was panicking even more, and didn't believe there was a proper airport or runway. The view from the window, which we could only glimpse through a stream of black smoke, revealed nothing but thick green forest. But here we were, descending rapidly into the jungle, then the plane flattened out and there was red earth flashing past the window and too fast a great bump and scraping onto something. And then we stopped. People were crying; they were happy too.

We drove from the airport for miles along what we were told was one of only two roads on the island and saw hardly any people. Those we did pass stopped to stare at our convoy of cars.

On our way to the hotel in the city of Kuching the lady sharing our car said, 'Thank God for the Aurora.' The Aurora Hotel was once an outpost of imperial luxury, and still retained some colonial elegance. When we arrived, my mother looked around it and decided it would do.

'Hmm, it is pretty dead, but at least we aren't! And we've been in worse places,' she said, with relief, which was true.

The hotel had high ceilings with whirring fans, a restaurant with tablecloths, and even a piano bar with a rather bad elderly crooner.

'Well, he ain't Dean Martin, and this sure ain't Caesar's Palace!' Audrey said. I liked it when she said 'ain't' as it sounded cheeky and as if we were in a film.

The BOAC staff were madly sorting out room, the hotel reception, and tea and sandwiches were provi... in the lounge area where someone from the airline made a speech saying that this was 'a very unusual incident' and had occurred because of a flock of migrating birds flying into the plane and damaging a propeller. He told us that flights were being laid on as soon as possible to take us on to Malaysia and every arrangement was being made 'for our safety and comfort'.

The following day we made one or two attempts to explore, but it was too hot and we soon came back to sit under a fan on the big leather chairs in the lounge with iced tea. Audrey was looking at me out of the corner of her eye, and I could tell it was one of her rare moments of self-doubt, as she embarked on something that might not be a good idea.

It was not a bad moment to ask a question.

'Who was Perry who gave you your pearls, and why wasn't he the real thing?' Our recent adventures were beginning to make us see a little more eye to eye. Our double act had survived this rackety life so far, and I was earning my stripes as a more equal member. Too much had been revealed, perhaps, over the Roger affair for her to treat me like a baby any more. It seemed that she was going to tell me.

'Perry was great fun. I suppose I thought that, as I'd lost my true love, the boy who I thought I'd marry, then I could at least have a good time,' I had heard Auntie Grace call her 'a good-time girl' once and been surprised as she didn't seem to be having a good time at all.

The glitter of social success might at least distract her from her grief at losing James, she had reasoned, and this dazzling life would, naturally, be provided by a man. If Britain didn't have Hollywood stars, it did have aristocrats, and the elusive glamour that my mother had yearned for, that she saw hanging around the heads of Hollywood actors like a gaudy halo, she also found in any title or upper crust name.

My mother's spells in London now showed her that there was a new bohemianism that disguised class. She might not make it in Mayfair, but she could have a go at Hampstead, and in bare feet. That spring of 1948 she was still only twenty-two, and she put aside her Forties suits and cocktail dresses for slouchy trousers and kicked off her shoes to dance with her new boyfriend Perry Guinness in jazz cellars and to lie on the grass on Hampstead Heath. It was a far cry from the chilly bedsit in Maida Vale and her still-piercing memories of James.

Post-war London was bombed, exhausted and poor. But the rich picked up their lives where they left off, and the country-house parties still had lavish meals, hunting and dancing till dawn, just as they had before the war. Perry called Audrey his 'little cutiepie' and took her everywhere with his 'crowd'. Her new flatmate, Heather, with whom she shared a Hampstead cottage, came along too. Heather was what Audrey called 'shabby posh'. She never used make-up or brushed her long blonde mane, and always wore the same old camel coat covered in the hair of her Labradors. Audrey quickly acquired an old camel coat and love of Labradors.

Her friend Duncan had an old pink car he called Mrs Frequently because of how often she broke down, and would take them on eccentric jaunts such as picnics in candlelit caves. He held all-night parties in his Bayswater flat at which Audrey met girls who smoked with long cigarette holders and said shocking things. Audrey added this early beatnik look to her own repertoire of styles.

Jazz musician George Melly sometimes came along to the parties, and he now helped Audrey to get a job at a new jazz venue called Club 11 in Great Windmill Street, taking tickets at the door. It was one of the first clubs playing bebop, and when she wasn't at the door selling tickets she could now climb the rickety staircase to the rehearsal room, to watch musicians like Ronnie Scott and Johnny Dankworth let rip with this urgent and thrilling new music. In the afternoons they'd sit in the dingy club listening to George Melly, in his zoot suit, unleashing a storm of hilarious and wicked anecdotes.

This bohemian scene was distracting her from her broken heart, and at the weekends there were visits to big country houses, where Audrey learnt to mingle with Perry's baronet cousins and their wealthy friends. As she copied Heather's casual style, pulling on wellington boots and going on bracing walks after long Sunday lunches, then curling up in front of log fires to read *Country Life*, it appeared that she had successfully buried her Liverpool working-class past. Her gift for mimicry made her seem one of them and her gift for storytelling earned her a place at the dinner table.

But she knew that it was only because she was on the arm of Perry that she had access to this exclusive club. When they weren't in Soho jazz clubs they were in the houses of his friends in Park Lane and Mayfair. It was the life she had dreamt of and the pain of James was at last receding, so why had she suddenly realized that it wasn't the real thing?

I had a feeling that the story stopped here because it involved my father, and I knew that one day I would have to ask her some difficult questions but that the right moment hadn't arrived. She now talked about him very little and this saddened me but I wanted her to mention him first, not me. I thought of him every night before I went to sleep, and again every morning when I woke up, but it felt like my secret, and for now I simply hugged the memories quietly to myself. One day I would ask, but not just yet.

15

Pearl of the Orient

I REMEMBER THE HEAT, and the cycle rickshaws, and the deafening roar of surf on a white sand beach. I remember monkeys with tufty beards and their babies clinging to their middles, a snake temple and a man seated on the ground with a python around his shoulders. I remember red Chinese letters and a sign saying PRECIOUS PAGODA and the yellow of the pagoda towers behind. I remember the funicular up Penang Hill and big colonial villas with dusty gardens and cool rooms, sparsely furnished with bamboo furniture.

Or do I? How much of these memories comes from photographs shown to me on our return I'm not sure. Back in Southport there would be the darkened lounge, the glow of an electric fire, and the endless slide shows with the click of the carousel turning and the Kodak colour images popping up on the screen, as my mother relived our travels as if they were just extended holidays. Of course the audience might only be Auntie Grace and Uncle Phil, sitting a little tight-lipped and disapproving with their very small glasses of sherry, so it was probably wise of her to play things down.

This process normalized the experience, and turned us into intrepid tourists rather than the desperate pair we really were. 'There's Sally at the old fort. Oh and look, there's Sally with the monkeys at the botanical gardens.'

I have freckles and pudgy legs and smile and smile for the camera. 'And there's Uncle Les getting us a rickshaw.' Friends of my mother who got past the acquaintance stage were always given the prefix Uncle and Auntie to make my use of their first name sound more polite. She had heard someone refer to me as 'precocious' and this alarmed her. It may have threatened her idea of me as her innocent little companion.

We had stayed for some time in 'Uncle Les's' villa up on a leafy hillside, but I slept in a guesthouse in the garden. He must have been a boyfriend, a lover, but I had no sense that they were in any way 'in love'. My mother would say that you didn't just kiss a frog and he magically turned into a prince; that was just a fairy story. In real life you kissed a frog and then 'set your mind into turning him into a prince', but it was hard to imagine how much effort it would take in the case of Les. He was a pleasant man, friendly, but impossible to remember when you weren't actually with him. Even looking at the cine films or photographs later, it was difficult to recall anything about him. Poor Roger from the cruise was memorable, and I could even recollect George from the Kill Devil Hills for his sad awkwardness. But Les never said or did anything to surprise you, although my mother would tell people that Les was quite the life and soul of the party. His house was very big, so he must have been rich, and he didn't need to go to his office every day as he owned the company, so he could play golf and go to the club and give parties where he could be the life and soul.

I once again began to feel terribly trapped and with a growing fear that this could be for ever. There were peacocks in the garden of his house whose strangled miaow was the first sound of the morning, and I woke up to it feeling hot and marooned. A Chinese lady called an ayah looked after me, but didn't speak very good English and our time together was uncomfortable for both of us. Time moved slowly as my panic grew.

Yet again I was saved by a story. One desultory afternoon in the shady lounge of the Penang Club, I turned on the big black and white TV in the corner to discover that among the Chinese and Malay programmes there were American TV shows. After the advertisements for Ovaltine or Tiger Balm, there suddenly appeared a beautiful blonde, swooping out of the star-filled sky on a broomstick, to thrillingly zingy Sixties music. She flew by, writing in glittering stars the word *Bewitched*. She then popped into her kitchen and, with a twitch of her nose, turned her witch's hat into a frying pan, kissed her bemused husband, became a cat and jumped into his arms to become the adorable Samantha again.

Bewitched was a blast of the America I had hoped we would find when we visited New York, or Kitty Hawk, or Palm Springs, but we never quite did. The series was set in a place we never visited: a sun-drenched suburbia of happy families with bright modern homes and perfect lawns. Samantha, who I adored to the point of pleading to change my name to hers, was both all-powerful and deliciously lovable.

But this TV Samantha was a witch, something my mother often claimed to be and had made our special secret. Samantha's mother tells her that they are quicksilver, a fleeting shadow, and that they live on the wind and in the sparkle of a star. It was exactly the magic that my mother longed for – a superpower that would set her apart from mere mortals with their dull routine lives – but she seemed to wiggle her nose and nothing happened.

The show offered an interesting insight into marriage. Samantha's husband was handsome and fun and she loved him; but he was also the butt of the joke. It seemed as if he should be in control, with his important job in an advertising agency and lots of money, but whenever he tried to command his wife to stop using her magic she just gave a wicked laugh and played another trick on him. If I couldn't be Samantha, then I longed to be Tabitha, their pretty baby daughter who had such a seemingly normal, happy home, but also a mother who could do anything just by twitching her nose.

When I challenged my mother about it, and asked her to prove her bewitching powers, she twitched and wiggled her nose quite convincingly, but then said it was against the witches' code to use magic just to make a point.

'Hey,' she said, changing the subject, 'why don't angry witches ride their broomsticks?'

I just shook my head.

'They're afraid of flying off the handle!' she said, trying to get me to play; but I wasn't going to laugh. I felt like telling her that Samantha appeared to be able to make her husband do anything she wanted, unlike my mother's boyfriends who seemed to fail us constantly.

MY MOTHER HAD MET LES at the Penang Club, where she briefly had a job in the office. It was a sprawling place along the seafront with gardens and a swimming pool where I liked to swim. Children were only allowed during certain hours, though, and the rest of the time I spent at the guesthouse reading next to a fan and waiting for the day to end. I would be taken out in the cooler evenings, bought ice cream, but I remember feeling choked with unhappiness and not knowing why.

When she wasn't working or with Uncle Les, we explored George Town and took rickshaws to a temple. We visited a night market where giant moths bashed themselves against outdoor lamps and tortoises crawled in boxes. There were picnics, snake charmers, monkeys and a children's party where I didn't know anyone but I won at Pass the Parcel.

How long we stayed and why we left is not clear, but I know that there were rows and tears. I watched several episodes of *Bewitched*, counting off the days till the next instalment each week, so we were there for quite some time. At last she began to answer questions: yes, she did really like Uncle Les, but no, she wasn't in love, and no we weren't going to stay too much longer. She loved something called the 'lifestyle' but not the bluff businessman who might provide it.

As we travelled down Penang Hill on the creaky old funicular she looked across the hillside with its waving palm trees and said, her face swollen with weeping, 'Why can't I be like Nellie – you know, in *South Pacific*? She falls in love at first sight with Peter Finch, this romantic handsome French- man, and just lives happily ever after.'

So this was our *South Pacific* moment, rather than our *Bewitched* moment, and it hadn't worked out, so we moved on to Cairo.

SABET SABESCUE was a snake, a fat phallic draught excluder, which I kept on my bed. His glittering glass eyes reminded me of his namesake and, in that naive way of young girls, I would wrap around him, my legs either side of his furry sausage shape. I don't remember when or where I got him, only that I loved him and so gave him that name to remind me of the real Sabet, who was a much more elusive creature. The real Sabet was a man in Cairo whose smile remained, like the Cheshire cat, long after the rest of him had vanished. Sabet's gleeful grin hovers at the edge of my memory, along with the thrill of driving too fast in his open car with the wind in my hair.

Cairo had been a disaster before I found him. We were staying in the worst hotel we had ever stayed in; there were pools of water on the lino floor which we had to step over, and it was right next to the mosque whose muezzin woke us at dawn, along with a chorus of barking dogs. My mother was panicking. I had terrible stomach ache and was curled up under the fan all day.

The room reeked of the hubba-bubba pipe from the grubby café below, a smell that drifted over the entire city as it sucked and bubbled its sweet smoke all around us. The parks were full of it, as young men gathered to obliterate the gentle scent of jasmine and orange blossom that would otherwise have floated on the hot night breeze. It was everywhere we went, filling the big restaurant boat on the Nile where we had dinner, even enveloping the graceful felucca with the billowing sails that we took down the river past fields and farms.

The only scent more powerful was Sabet's heady cologne. I have smelt it sometimes on a passing stranger and stopped them to ask its name but never found it out. Later research suggests it had a base of ylang-ylang with notes of black pepper to offset its sultry sweetness. Even a hint of these ingredients takes me back to that time and the heightened awareness I had in his presence.

I first smelt that scent of his as I approached the bar. I couldn't say my usual line to him – about looking after my mother for me while I went to bed – as we were staying in our squalid hotel, I knew that we couldn't have afforded to stay even one night in this palace. It was like something from the *Arabian Nights*, and we loved the gardens with their glowing lanterns and a buzz of chatter from the wealthy young Egyptians who gathered here after dusk. My mother was sitting at a table among the palm trees with the luminous pool beyond her.

So I just smiled at the man hopefully, saying, 'Hello, I'm Sally,' and he turned to me and flashed that dazzling smile of his. I realized that he was too young for my mother, but very handsome and brimming with fun.

'Hello, Miss Sally.' He shook my hand and gave a mock bow. 'I am Sabet Sabescue, and from this moment your faithful servant.'

The barman returned with our drinks and crisps on a small tray, but Sabet plonked his own drink down on our tray and picked it up, saying, 'Please, allow me,' and followed me over to my mother.

He bowed to her. 'Madame, this small English rose appeared beside me, and I had to see for myself the radiant beauty of her mother.' Audrey raised an eyebrow and I could see she thought this was a bit much; but then his friends arrived with shouts, and they greeted him as if he had just won a football match. He was so much their hero, and they were so happy to see him, that my mother couldn't resist. They all joined our table, and soon we were part of that excited buzz and the sweet haze of the hubba-bubba pipe was swirling around us too.

Sabet had an office with one entire wall that was a giant tank of glowing tropical fish swimming among coral and a sunken wreck. It had a big dining table where his secretary brought us an Egyptian breakfast of ful medames, a stew of warm beans with cumin and garlic served on smoky char-grilled flatbreads.

His desk was huge and shiny with lots of toys on it. One was a magic ball, which you could ask any question, then turn it over and the answer could be viewed through a glass window. The answers were things like 'It is decidedly so!' or 'Outlook not so good'. He would ask it questions for me, such as, 'Is Sally the cutest girl in the world?' then read out, 'It is very certain.'

He drove us around in a big white open-top car, and wore dark sunglasses that he called his 'gogs'. His nationality wasn't clear; he had a faintly American accent, but was part-Greek, part-Asian, part-Egyptian, did business mostly in the Middle East, and his friends were mostly Russian. He was somehow too much, too young; his smile too dazzling, his confidence too exuberant. He mesmerized my mother and her pragmatism vanished. Perhaps he had saved us. Before we met him there was clearly an awful problem, and I tried to understand what it was. The awful hotel made me think it was money, so I tried to suggest that we could sell my Miss Gillette ring. She gave me one of her cool looks, and I knew that her wails of 'What shall we do?' were not ever meant to be actually answered, least of all by me.

But a solution must have been found, for we were suddenly piling our bags into Sabet's car and moving into a hotel that was terribly fancy. We had a huge cool room with a comfortable sitting area with sofas and a TV. My mother told me that she had to go somewhere for a day or two; a chambermaid was booked to look after me, and the hotel doctor came to look at my stomach ache. He checked on me every day, while the chambermaid sat and watched TV on the sofa – it was in Arabic so I just read my books.

After two or three days I started to panic. My stomach was better and I could go down and sit by the pool, but I didn't know where my mother was. I had always felt safe in the belief that she would stay away no longer than the number of days she had told me she would, but this time I felt a force stronger than her love for me was at work and I was frightened that something had gone wrong or I had been forgotten. I'm not sure how long it was, but it was certainly some days later before she finally appeared. I was furious, and asked her where on earth she had been. She said she had just been to see the Pyramids.

Later, when Sabet drove us out of the gates and down the dusty road to the town, I looked back to see the sign and realized that the hotel was called Hilton Pyramids and that the Pyramids were clearly right there beside us.

We stayed on for some time, and most days we'd go with Sabet to his favourite Gezira Club, where he loved to hang out as he knew people there. I would be sent to sit by what he called the Lido, which was a swimming pool with a bridge over it. It was always empty and had big leaves and purple flowers floating on the surface, fallen from the trees over-head. When it was quiet, after lunch, large black crows sat on the tables around the pool in the grey muggy heat, which made it feel creepy. I would wander into the old-fashioned clubhouse with its dark red walls and big chairs and find somewhere cool to sit and read.

That was when we took the felucca down the Nile. My mother had said it would be romantic, and an adventure. We drifted along through the warm air, the water lapping as the boat sailed along, but we didn't seem to be going anywhere. It reminded me of one of my favourite books, *The Mill on the Floss*, when Maggie drifts down the river, too tired to stop the boat. We all seemed hot and tired and relieved just to be

Mum, left, with friends.

moving along. Sabet was restless, though, and got annoyed with the man sailing the boat. He didn't like to be taken anywhere; he liked to be the taker. My mother was quieter than I'd ever known her and she hadn't sung any of her songs for ages.

'Why didn't the Pyramids have doorbells?' I tried.

She shrugged.

'Cos they had horns, so you could just toot an' come in!' I said with a theatrical flourish, 'Tut-an-kham-un! Get it?' Sabet laughed, but she only gave me a weak smile.

I pretended to be loving it all, with the felucca's big white sails ballooning out above us and pretty cushions to lie back on. Sabet cheered up then, and told me one of his stories. It was about Osiris, the god of the dead, who was killed by his brother, and his body was cut up into pieces. His wife had to put him back together again to have a baby with him. He still didn't come back to life, but he lived on in an under-world of shadows, and the ancient Egyptians thought that this river was his world, with its dark murky depths. We looked down into the waters drifting by and imagined a lost world of these people with their myths and stories. Sabet's stories were different from my mother's. My mother's were often about her, and about people she knew and places she had been. Sabet's stories were about mystery and magic.

Sabet had many moods and you never knew which one he would be in, or when it would end and he would change again. He could be quiet and mysterious, but at other times fun, childish and full of mad games. He was terribly gen-erous, so I stopped saying I liked things in case he bought them for me and my mother got annoyed. He had already given me a lovely dress with a sparkly cape for my shoulders and a scented sandalwood jewellery box. He paid for me to have a manicure and pedicure at the hotel beauty salon, and laughed when I screamed as the lady rubbed a cheese grater on the soles of my feet. He helped choose which colour nail varnish I should have; when I couldn't decide, he said, 'When you grow up you'll learn: you have to suffer to be beautiful.'

He would put an arm around me and say, 'Me, I love kids!' and then forget about me again. I didn't usually mind when grown-ups did that, but with Sabet I minded a lot and wanted him to like me, even though he didn't really listen when I tried to tell him things. Then suddenly he was going away for a while on business, and promised to meet us once more in England where we would 'get together in Swinging London and have some fun!' We never saw him again.

16

A Cold New Year

TRAVELLING WITH MY MOTHER played unsettling tricks with my sense of time. There would be so many endless days and weeks when nothing happened and then, when I was least expecting it, life would speed up and we would be tumbling down another rabbit hole. This was one of those moments, which found us hastily packing our bags, walking up the steps to the BOAC plane in warm muggy air and looking back at swaying palm trees in the early-morning light. Then, only hours later, we were on the other side of the world, in the wintry north of England, driving through a cold grey afternoon with the street lights already lit, and small plastic Christmas trees winking from living-room windows.

So there we were, back in Southport in the cold, unloved and unlived-in house, rifling through drawers looking for my woolly tights and duffel coat, unwrapping my painted cat ornament from Sarawak and setting it down beside Sabet's jewellery box on my dressing table. Even the funny brown paper that his present was wrapped in still smelt of

Cairo and was coated in the city's soft sweet dust. As usual my mother went out and I went through to the Back Flat, to say hello to the housekeeper, show her my souvenirs, and eat egg and chips to the sounds of Hughie Green on *Opportunity Knocks*.

For my mother the grim spectre of Christmas was now looming, too awful to mention. I was excited to be back in the wintry cosiness, and longed for a really Christmassy Christmas, but it was hard to imagine how it could be achieved. I think that the idea of the two of us alone in that house was as unthinkable to her as for me. So letters had been posted, phone calls were being made, and another plan had emerged. She was suddenly triumphant and back in business. Now we were rushing out to buy smart new outfits and fancy Christmas presents like leather driving gloves in a man's size.

It seemed that she had known Vernon Lilford from his visits to Southport, where he had partied with Peter Cooper's crowd, and now, as a widow, she had hopes of getting to know him better. Vernon had inherited a title and estate at the age of eighteen, and became the 7th Baron Lilford, a title which brought an ancestral home, Heskin Hall, in the Lancashire countryside, but no fortune to go with it. He had lived for some years in South Africa where he manufactured car tyres, but still managed to spend quite a bit of time in England leading the playboy lifestyle popular in the Sixties, accessorized with E-Type Jags and dolly birds.

Audrey had reason to believe that his marriage to Muriel, or 'Mu', was not going well. It was his fourth marriage, and his friends were now putting it around town that he would soon be free again. One had hinted that my mother could perhaps be the fifth Lady Lilford and that Vernon had said Christmas at Heskin Hall would be a chance for him and Audrey to get to know each other better.

My mother told me that it would be a perfect Christmas, in a stately home, with real log fires and grand dinners and lots of other children for me to play with.

We drove through the flat, wet Lancashire country-side and it was growing dark when we went up a sweeping driveway to the heavy doors of a Tudor manor house that reminded me of the box for the game of Cluedo. The dark oak-panelled Great Hall had a huge Christmas tree, and the sitting room beyond with its leather sofas and log fires did feel properly Christmassy. But it felt very grown up, with a lot of strangers smelling of whisky and no one my age in sight. Vernon greeted us warmly, and someone led me upstairs to meet the children. I looked anxiously at my mum but she said 'Scoot and skidaddle' cheerfully and waved me off.

We walked along a corridor to another part of the house that was called the 'nursery wing'. Here the various offspring of the guests bickered and fought each other overseen by a nanny. It seemed that we were having our own Christmas here, with separate meals, and it immediately brought back the old feeling of panic that going to school had given me. This was worse, as I seemed to be expected to stay here day and night, and to even sleep in a room with some of these children.

After begging to see my mother I was taken into the dining room, where the long table was laid in splendour with candelabras and holly, and the guests in evening dresses were laughing and talking loudly. I whispered to my mother that I wanted to be with her, and she at last gave in and said that I could sleep in her room and she would be up later so I should go to bed now.

I was then taken to her room – now our room – and left there. This would have been a relief, but while I was getting my night things together in the children's wing, one of the older boys had told me that I was very brave to leave the safety of this wing at all. He warned me that Heskin Hall was a famously haunted house and that the bedrooms I was going to were wandered at night by the ghost of a poor Catholic girl; Cromwell's soldiers had hung her by her neck from the ceiling beams and then cut down her body and let it drop into the lime pit below. She could pass through walls and walked to and fro, moaning softly. I said he was making it up, but he then brought me a book and showed me the part that confirmed the whole story, with dates and pictures of Cromwell and the house.

I therefore lay in bed in a cold sweat with the sheets over my head, counting the moments till my mother came. I had put my stocking at the end of the bed as my mother had told me to, but realized that Santa was unlikely to risk meeting a moaning ghost and it was probably going to be empty in the morning. I sensed that the whole Christmas was a disaster.

It felt like hours before I heard someone or something coming into the room. I didn't dare look in case it was Santa or a ghost, or just my mother. There was no moaning, so I told myself it couldn't be the poor ghost girl. I heard rustling, and then at last what I knew was my mother getting into bed, and I finally dared to emerge from the suffocating bedding and listen for the sound of her breathing. I at last fell asleep in a lather of anxious sweat.

In the morning, I was relieved to see that brave Santa had come anyway. He had left me a couple of exciting gifts: a perfume-making kit and a Magic Fingers automatic knitting machine. I loved to make things and had tried to teach myself to knit, but my mother hadn't been able to help and I had never worked it out. Now the box showed a scarf half made and it promised 'A Row a Second'. Santa must have known that I loved perfume, so the perfume kit was the perfect present, with all kinds of interesting devices, like rubber droppers and test tubes to measure things to 'mix beautiful bouquets and aromas'.

I carried it with me to the dreaded nursery wing, hoping to find a quiet corner to try it out. At breakfast the squabbling had turned into fierce showing off, as the children sat at the long table displaying their presents to each other and shooting jealous looks at the things their siblings, half-siblings and step-siblings had been given.

I managed to find a quiet corner but was sorry to see that the perfume kit said that an adult must assist. Although the knitting machine instructions didn't say this in so many words, it was clearly the case after I had spent a long time puzzling over diagrams and tussling with balls of wall and hooks.

At last we were allowed to go down to the grown-ups and I showed my mother the boxes, but she frowned and said that we would examine them properly when we got home. I noticed that whenever I talked to my mother, Vernon looked at me as if he wished I would go away. I didn't take it to heart as he looked at the other children this way too but I felt anxious and panicky about how to get through the rest of the visit.

There was one nice man who asked me my name and asked if he could see my presents. He said his name was Mick and he had only been given soap on a rope in his stocking so I had done much better. He said that he wasn't too good at knitting but wondered if he could help with the perfume as it looked very interesting.

We went off and found an empty billiard room with a small table where we could set up our perfume factory. He got out the little stands for the test tubes and put the glass tubes in so it looked like a proper laboratory. He then read out all the names of the bottles. There were the undiluted fragrance oils, then there were the dilutants, and the mixing beakers. The oils had lovely names like tuberose, jasmine and lily of the valley, and the items for mixing and making had interesting names like pipettes, vials and atomisers. Best of all was a beautiful frosted bottle to put your favourite finished perfume into, with a label with flowers on it and a space to write the name of the scent.

We mixed away all morning. We concocted a face cream in a pot with geranium and lavender, which he said would keep my skin as soft and lovely as it was now. We made roll-on scents with citrus aromas, and finally we made a delicious perfume for the big frosted bottle. It took time to find the perfect mix. Mick said he was learning a lot about scents: what was floral, or musky, or light and citrusy. We kept adding a little of this or that just because we loved the name, like palmarosa which he said made him think of Spanish señoritas. Then there were small slips of paper to dip in and sniff. At last we poured our perfect scent into the lovely bottle and he held down the label while I wrote the name we had agreed on, which was my name: Sally. He sang a song, 'Sally, Sally, Pride of our Alley', and said they should use that for the TV ad to sell the perfume. It was the happiest time I'd had for as long as I could remember and the day still comes back to me more vividly than almost any other memory. It must have been a reawakening of the contentment I'd felt 'helping' in my father's workshop.

When I told my mother where I'd been and what I'd been doing, she laughed and told all the grown-ups. Everyone thought it was very funny because Mick was a famous wrestler, Mick McManus, and not the sort of person who would make perfume with little girls. The perfume making became a running joke, along with something Mick was supposed to have said on television, which was 'not the ears, not the ears', and my mother would mimic him, saying 'not the ears' as I dragged him off by his ears to play with me.

After that I made the billiard room my den, taking my books there and a blanket to curl up with. I wore my perfume, ate sweets and managed to feel all right. My mother agreed that the perfumes were very good and wore the one called Sally, which she said was as lovely as me.

The next day was 'the hunt' and my mother said she loved tradition. We went out in our coats to watch the men in red and black jackets mount their horses, then a man took around a tray of drinks. There were lots of dogs barking and running about, and then the huntsmen blew their horn and they all clattered off down the broad driveway. My mother had disappeared and when I finally found her she and Vernon were in a room having an intense chat and she asked me to wait outside. I knew that this was a crucial turning point in our mission. We had searched at least two or three of the four corners of the earth and not found our saviour, but I was now frightened that my mother might have convinced herself that this red-faced man who didn't like me could be 'the one'.

Back in our room, my mother sat with her heated Carmen rollers in to try to get her hair to flick up at the ends. She said that country damp made everyone look terrible. I could see that she was unhappy. She told me that we had been invited to stay for New Year's Eve as there would be a big party. I knew she hoped I would say that I wanted to go home, perhaps so that she could argue with me, so I didn't say anything.

The next day she told me that she had decided not to stay for New Year's Eve after all. She said Vernon had made it clear that if they were married then they would have to spend some of the time in South Africa and travelling, and he insisted that I would have to go to a boarding school.

It felt like a brush with the greatest horror I could imagine. I thought of my misery at day school, and then imagined it night and day, for weeks on end and with no escape. It seemed like quite the worst thing I could think of. We trailed back to Southport, my mother suspiciously quiet, and the car windows open to let out the overpowering scent of Sally, which I had rather liberally daubed onto my wrists and neck. I thought about my lucky escape and for some weeks afterwards I dreaded hearing Vernon's name, just in case he had convinced her of his horrible plan. But he was never mentioned again.

'DO YOU THINK I look like Millicent Martin?' my mother asked Auntie Ava as we sat having coffee.

'Who's Millicent Martin?' I asked, interrupting, which they didn't like.

'She's on the television, she's funny.'

'Oh yes, you do look quite like her!' said Auntie Ava generously.

Then Mummy whispered something, and I heard her say, 'Ronnie was married to her . . .'

The first time Ronnie Carroll came over to our house I realized straight away he was the best sort of grown-up: in fact, hardly grown up at all. My mother was out, and Mrs Braithwaite from the Back Flat was putting her feet up. The man who had rung the bell just strolled in when I opened the door, saying, 'Hello there, you must be the famous Sally!' which was unusual, as some of Audrey's friends didn't know my name. He asked if my mother was home and introduced himself as Ronnie. Then, without asking, he made himself at home, pouring a drink and looking through my mother's record collection in the cabinet. I asked him if he was hungry and if he would like some of my cake. He said that he'd love that, so I went off to get some for him.

I'd just raided Mrs Braithwaite's cupboards to make my 'cake', which was really a mixture of her breakfast cereal and some coloured sprinkles I'd found called Hundreds and Thousands. Then I'd used a few other sweet things to make it stick together. I had only done this while looking for food colouring for the love potions I was creating. Mrs B had said to look through her baking cupboard, though why she had one when she never baked I wasn't sure. But it had so many interesting items that I had got into a creative frenzy.

I came back with a tray of the 'cake' and a love potion. I'd added cochineal to the potion so it was a wonderful pink, with rose petals and leaves floating in it.

Ronnie said it all looked yummy and tucked in. As he was munching he showed me a record and said that it was his twin brother on the cover, and asked me who was the more handsome. I knew it was him, but I said that the man on the cover had even bigger teeth than he did. Ronnie had huge smiley teeth, and he laughed at that and sang me a song from the record, 'Ring-a-Ding Girl', and said that his twin had sung it at the Eurovision Song Contest.

He drank his love potion and threw himself back on the sofa, saying he was now in love with the whole world, and me in particular as I was his Ring-a-Ding Girl. I said that the love potion didn't work for little girls, but would work for the first lady he saw. At that moment Mrs B put her head around the door, and after she had gone we both burst

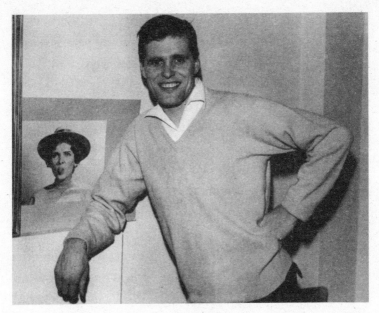

Ronnie Carroll.

out laughing. He said my potion had failed, but then we heard my mother's car, Bluebird as we called it, coming up the drive and Audrey jumped out. Ronnie went down on his knees and said he was hopelessly in love, as a small witch had forced him to drink a powerful potion. My mother seemed very pleased, and went off to get ready so they could go out to dinner.

She brought him into my room with her to say, 'Night night,' and he even looked at my books and tucked me in. I went to sleep wishing she would marry him.

The next day he had gone, but my mother said we would be visiting him in London where he had a mews house. At morning coffee with Auntie Ava she seemed very excited and talked about him a lot. She had met him at the Prince when he was up for a while to play golf with some pals. She said his best friends were Sean Connery, Peter Cook and Bruce Forsyth, that he had been married to Millicent Martin who was a big TV personality, and that everybody said she looked very like Millicent as they had the same red hair.

The only problem with Ronnie was that he was a hell-raiser and a gambler. He had once flown to Las Vegas and gambled twenty thousand pounds away in a couple of hours, leaving only enough for his cab fare back to the airport to fly home. She said that he really liked children, as though that was a very strange thing; that his career was a bit on the skids and that he blamed the Beatles. It was hard to tell from this information whether they were likely to get married or not.

A couple of weeks later we went down to London and visited his mews house near Park Lane. It had a white grand piano which he played and he gave me the words to a song, 'You Say Tomato, I Say Tomato', and I sang along. Then he burst out laughing and said I'd done it all wrong, and you had to say 'tomato' in different accents each time. He showed me and we all sang 'You say tomayto and I say tomaaato' and it was great fun. Then he took us to an Italian restaurant where he taught me to wind spaghetti around my fork and how to talk in a silly Italian accent. When Audrey was telling him stories I could help her, as she could check things like 'What was that hotel in Borneo?' or 'Was that our man in Cairo, or our man in Palm Springs?' and then I could add funny things of my own. He loved it and said, 'You are quite a double act.' We were staying at a hotel nearby and he walked us back, then I went to bed while they sat in the bar downstairs.

I was horribly disappointed the next morning when my mother took me to a nursery school in Knightsbridge, saying that although it was for babies I was to stay there for a while, as she had to do some shopping. The girls who were working there said that I could be their helper, but I didn't believe and knew that I was just being treated like one of the much younger children. I was choked with unhappiness all day surrounded by toddlers, and at times could hardly breathe. I steadied myself by looking forward to the evening and seeing Ronnie. When she finally came they were closing up and the staff had to wait for her, and she hadn't even bought anything on the shopping trip. She then announced I was to have another babysitter for the evening so they didn't take me with them and the whole trip was spoiled. On the train on the way home I asked when we would see Ronnie again and she said he was working on a cruise ship for a while, so she hoped to see him after that. We never did.

MY MOTHER'S HUNT – our hunt – for love seemed to be failing. We had travelled so far, and I had watched her trying so hard, that it was beginning to be too painful to think of her searching any further. I remembered something that my friend Humphrey had said on our cruise, when he had sighed and said, 'Divine Discontent.' And that if you really wanted to find love it was closer than you imagined. What had he meant?

My mother had always shown a brazen confidence about almost anything, so it was a shock when I first saw, as a small child, that this could vanish in an instant. There came a day when we were walking down Lord Street and she stopped dead and quietly drew us into a doorway. She didn't speak, and the air around us, usually charged with her bright glamour, suddenly dimmed. She had seen something to make her tremble, and we turned back from our outing and went straight home, where she vanished into her room.

As I grew older I understood that this was a danger: the sight of James Leadsom with his wife and children.

She always believed that he was the love of her life and with him everything would have been different, and she would have been different. Was this holding us back? One afternoon we watched *Gone with the Wind* again, and I saw Scarlett's fantasy of love for the unlikely and inspid Ashley, and how this illusion had blinded her to any other love. Was this what Humphrey meant, when he suggested that something was just always in the way? And why had she married my father and had she loved him? This was perhaps the most important question of all, but who could I ask?

17

The Midnight Kiss

AVA HAD TWIN BEDS, pushed close together with lace cascading down from the ceiling to hang in drapes around the bedheads, and piles of satin pillows. She patted the bed beside her for me to join her, and put the television on. My mother was at the dentist, and our housekeeper was away, so I'd been left with Auntie Ava. She had changed into a frilly frothy dressing gown although it was not long after lunch, and we were in her even frillier frothier bedroom. Anthony had his own bedroom in dark manly colours. He came up with a silver tray of tea for her, as he did every afternoon, and she poured us both a cup, then took a bottle from under the bed and poured some of it into her cup.

'How long have you been Mummy's friend?' I asked her.

'Oh golly, years and years, darling. Since the dinosaurs were roaming about, anyway.'

'So did you know her when she met my daddy?' I asked hopefully.

'Yes, your daddy was a lovely man. It was a tragedy, the whole thing. Very sad.'

'How did Mummy meet him?'

Gradually, as the afternoon wore on, I got a more full description of those events than my mother had ever offered me. Ava had never had a guarded tongue, or much awareness of children, so she simply told me what she could remember, with no thought for her audience at all.

'She met Neil, your daddy, when she was a beauty queen and he took some photographs for her. It was that awful summer after she got back from America; she was terribly unhappy, never really got over it. But, you know your mum, "best foot forward" and all that, so she did that competition down at the Sea Bathing Lake. It was quite a big thing, the English Rose Beauty Contest – girls from all over Britain went in for it. The girls would walk down the steps in an afternoon dress and long gloves, then parade around the circuit of the lake carrying a card that showed their number, smiling at the crowds and panel of judges.'

I knew that my mother could smile for England. First her eyes began to dance with laughter, then the joy of it spread across her heart-shaped face and became huge and radiant. She held back nothing, and gave you her whole self in a way that was hard to resist. And of course she knew that she would win; after all, she had been crowned Queen of the May every summer of her childhood, so her belief in divine right was unshakeable.

By the end of that afternoon she was handed the English Rose crown and sash, as Ava described it all, looking gleeful, any self-doubt vanquished.

Mum as Miss English Rose, 1950s.

She now needed pictures of herself to enter into other contests, and her friend Jean passed on the number of someone she knew who was a keen amateur photographer. The photographer was Neil McNicoll, my father, who turned up to meet Audrey at the beach and spent a sunny afternoon snapping pictures of her as she ran and skipped down sand dunes in her bikini, with her hair flying out behind her. I loved these images, with one hand held behind her head in a carefree gesture, and a sweet smile.

The contest that she had set her heart on was Miss Isle of Man. It held the promise of two things that she longed for: the first was travel, if only in this case a ferry across to Douglas, the island's capital; and the second was meeting interesting people.

In this case the interesting person was Geoff Duke, a handsome motorbike racing champion and hero of the Isle of Man TT Races, who was to be a judge of the contest. She had seen photographs of him and was determined to get there.

She would pull out triumphantly the photograph of the results of that beauty pageant. It showed a row of contestants – tall, leggy, shapely girls who look like proper beauty queens. But wearing the Miss Isle of Man sash and beaming up at Geoff Duke is a small impish girl several inches shorter than the other entrants. Audrey would giggle, pointing out that it was more about her 'personality' and other attributes than just having long legs, and that getting to know the judges well made a big difference!

Ava laughed to herself at this, and then continued.

Back in Southport, Neil had been in touch, asking her to meet up again, but she was already off to live in London and she met Perry Guinness soon afterwards. On visits home to Southport to visit her mother she would sometimes see Neil, and was aware that his eyes always followed her at any party. On one of these visits, now engaged to Perry, Audrey bumped into Neil again, and she was shocked to see him looking so ill and drawn.

Neil had been to Africa during his service in the RAF and had been very sick with malaria. It wasn't just the disease itself that made him so ill, but other complications and an overdose of drugs that he had accidentally been given at a makeshift RAF hospital. This had badly affected his immune system and liver, and he was now undergoing tests to work out a treatment plan.

Neil wasn't like the other, more fun-loving people that Audrey hung around with: he was very direct and open, always totally absorbed by whatever he was doing, whether it was taking photographs, or making furniture or films; and he would talk with excitement about books he was reading, or art and culture. She didn't know anyone quite like him. He now begged her to have dinner with him and, feeling sorry for him and flattered by the look in his eyes, she agreed, but only after explaining that she was engaged to Perry Guinness, of the well-known Guinness family.

She was taken aback when Neil, dropping her home after a lovely evening, pulled her towards him and kissed her deeply and hungrily. There was an intensity in the sick boy that fascinated her. Over the following weeks he sent her passionate letters decorated with drawings of how he imagined her, her naked curves made less obviously erotic by the angel wings he added to the images.

She agreed to see him again over Christmas, and he asked her if she would spend New Year's Eve with him. She said that she had to be back down south, as Perry had invited her to a party at a country house that night. Neil asked her the name of the house and if he could come at midnight just to kiss her once and go away again. She thought he was joking and laughed it off.

It snowed heavily on the New Year's Eve of 1956. Audrey was getting ready for the big party and was feeling great anticipation about the coming year. It was certainly a coup, to have won the heart of Perry Guinness, an eligible man, and their married life would be the one of glamour and luxury she had always imagined. She may not have been deeply in love with Perry, but they had fun together; and the life they shared, with its social whirl of parties, dancing and theatres, kept at bay any other longings. They hadn't made love yet, but she assumed that he was being a gentleman and waiting till they were married and that side of things would work out. The last few years had been shadowed by her wretchedness over James, her lost love, but now she believed that she was finally headed for happiness.

That same day Neil sat on a bus for nine hours as it made its way down from Southport to Oxfordshire and towards the house where Audrey was partying. He got off, and walked down the long drive just before midnight. The party was in full swing, with everyone in evening dress, as the young man in his duffel coat waited by the door trying to get a note to Audrey. Finally she was interrupted on the dance floor and handed the note which said, 'Just one kiss at midnight? I'll be at the front door, Neil.'

As the dance music stopped, someone turned on the radio and announced that the midnight chimes were beginning. The first chime rang out, signalling the end of that year and the beginning of a new chapter. Audrey looked over at Perry, who was carousing with his friends, and then rushed off to find Neil waiting by the door.

He lit up at the sight of her.

'You idiot! Come in, it's freezing!' She tried to pull him into the party.

'No, just one kiss is all I need, to warm me up for 1957!' He closed his eyes.

Audrey laughed and gave him the kiss that he had come so far to taste.

She begged him once more to come in and get warm, but he just sloped off into the night, pink lipstick on his shirt, with a grin and a wave. Perry soon drew her back into the crowd with his 'Happy New Year, my sweetie pie' and a warm hug, then she danced with him till dawn.

A few weeks later she made her regular visit to Southport to see her mother. She found her bedroom filled with red roses, and propped on the mantelpiece was a note from Neil. He was asking her to come to his flat that weekend, just for a small party with some of his friends. He was keen for her to meet them, and wanted to show her his photographs and short films and the furniture he had made for the flat, as carpentry was his other love. It was hard to refuse, particularly knowing that he was so ill, and she agreed to go.

After an entertaining evening around the dinner table, she was determined to deliver the speech she had prepared about 'just being friends' before she went home. She had to wait till everyone was gone, and then she began to explain.

He ignored her carefully chosen words and simply pulled her towards him and kissed her.

Ava broke off the story here, remembering that she was telling a child, although she was quite aware that I was a child who knew a lot more about adult matters than most other children.

'Your mother is quite a passionate woman, and I think she and Perry were more chummy. So with Neil being so carried away, they ended up going to bed together.'

She said that Audrey knew immediately that it had been a terrible mistake. She liked Neil, and deeply sympathized with his situation. He was only still in his twenties, and it all seemed so unfair, but it had been wrong to lead him on. His romanticism had swept her along, and she had given in to the moment, but the last thing she needed was some poor ill boyfriend who wasn't James Leadsom. Nor was he wealthy or well connected; nor, most importantly of all, was she in love with him. Poor Neil; he looked white-faced with misery as she told him that she still intended to marry Perry that spring. She went back down to London to be with Perry, and knew that it was the right decision.

Three weeks later Neil's phone calls from Southport had become pressing. He needed to see her, and she too couldn't put off talking to him any longer. She went back to South-port to stay at her mother's, and met Neil in a coffee bar. She told him that there was something they had to discuss, as her period was late. He was quiet. He had his own news, which was that the latest prognosis from the hospital had been a shock; it had now been made clear to him that he would never be well again, he would at some point begin to deteriorate, and that his condition was almost certainly terminal.

He realized as a poor trainee accountant, who may soon be unable to work, he was now in no position to support a wife and child. He knew he was not what Audrey had been dreaming of. He knew he had been carried away the other night, and was distraught that he had made her pregnant in the face of this news. But she was the girl he had always wanted, from the first time he set eyes on her.

OVER THE FOLLOWING WEEKS she returned several times to the unremarkable terraced house, too terrified to go in and suffer the brutality of a backstreet abortion, but at the same time inconsolable at the thought of being stuck with a baby and a marriage she had never wanted, and to a dying man. She believed her life was practically over.

So, I was born.

THE STORY THAT was told to me that afternoon by Ava didn't hurt my feelings, and nor did her guileless repetition of my mother's horrified reaction to the idea of having a child, her tears and her protestation 'I don't want a baby'. After all, at this stage it was just 'a baby' and she didn't know it would turn out to be me, Sally, who she had then got to know and learnt to love. She had at least done what she was supposed to do, and got married to my daddy. I had never seen her be unkind to my father; her attitude was always gentle and her only sin was 'going out' a lot. I could see that she was probably doing her best. It was becoming more obvious that love mainly finds you, or is right there beside you when you were looking in all the wrong places. It might be just a sick young man, or a little girl who can't sing or dance.

None of this helped me to fathom where her hunt for love might take us next. If anything, she was more desperate than I had ever seen her.

Whatever had previously been hidden could be out in the open after my father had died. The boot of our Triumph Herald clanked with the boxes of whisky and champagne we delivered to local councillors: those with the power to help her set up more Miller's Betting Shops in streets where the residents were not pleased. Brown envelopes of cash were almost certainly passed across restaurant tables as a thank you.

She spent more time at the casino, having 'meetings'. A friend of Peter Cooper's had winked at me, with an arm around her: 'She's a bit of a gangster, you know, your mum!' It frightened me, as the gangsters in films had guns and shot people.

Auntie Grace had whispered to Uncle Phil that the betting shops at least might not be as bad as 'the other thing', but they still proved that my mother was 'cheap as chips'.

With my father gone, Peter Cooper was now around more than ever and Audrey was always busy arranging 'fun' for him and his friends.

But who were these 'girls' and what did they do? It would usually be one of the girls on the phone when my mother would talk in a low voice of 'arrangements': parties in Liverpool or Manchester, 'dates' with this person or that. I heard names – Jodie, Mandy, Trish, and others who were all in constant orbit around my mother and would go on these dates which she was arranging – and it gave me a funny feeling. The air of hushed tones and mystery around it all only fuelled my curiosity.

I sensed that these connections and the crowd she mixed with were putting us both beyond the pale. I felt so sad that she was never invited anywhere and she would lie crying on her bed when she couldn't get an invitation to anniversary parties, golf-club gala dinners or fundraising fashion shows with buffets. She would say crossly, 'The ladies are all scared that I'll pinch one of their husbands,' and I wondered if they were right.

There was a further problem, which was that she was too good at drawing people out, and too keen to give them advice. Often the men she helped by setting up a 'date' would find themselves telling her all the details of their unhappy marriages and darkest secrets, feeling that she wouldn't judge them. In Southport this trick had given her power, but it also added to her outcast status, as she knew exactly where all the bodies were buried.

Sometimes she would tell on someone, and whisper to one of the men she knew that 'Patti's husband spends a lot of time at Man to Man – if you know what I mean?' This was the clothes shop which was a hub for Southport's gay community. The men who worked at the shop were great friends of hers, and great gossips. I would sit on a high velvet stool at the counter listening to the chatter, and one of them always made me hot chocolate with a marshmallow on top. He'd taken me to see Marlene Dietrich at the local theatre and, at the end of the show, he and his friends all ran to throw roses onto the stage. I loved him and their stylish, cosy shop. Our visits there meant that Audrey knew most of the insider information, and there were several gay couples – men who had previously been married to women – whom she had introduced to each other. She would say, with some satisfaction, 'People should just be who they are and get on with it!'

Sometimes all this intimate information damned her, though. I overheard her tell Peter Cooper that Auntie Ava's husband, Anthony, didn't like her because she knew about his 'sex problem' and that he had paid one of her girls to 'lie naked beside him, but nothing happened'. Perhaps there were others who felt the same about her knowing about any 'problems' or particular tastes that they might have.

She had now made quite enough money to host her own parties and dinners, with her splendid dining room, but who would come? I saw ladies cross to the other side of Lord Street when they saw her walking along. She had been obsessed for years with something called the 51 Club, an exclusive social group of fifty-one of Southport's smartest ladies, which you could only join when someone left or died and you went up the waiting list. Every now and then my mother would say that some woman had moved away and now it must be her turn. She would telephone the chairwoman hopefully. The phone would go down and she would just sit there for a moment, her eyes glassy with tears; they had given the place to another lady who had been below her on the list, or they had given it to someone who was a new arrival in Southport. So it went on for years, but she refused to give up. It was so unkind when she had been on the list so long, but whatever it was, they just thought she wasn't good enough. I would watch her as she got up from the telephone, wiping her eyes.

When we returned from our travels, I had wished and hoped life would become more normal, but I knew that we didn't fit in. We were somehow not quite right, we were just slightly 'off'. Worst of all, I was beginning to realize that I was turning into as much an outsider as she was.

18

The Young Eve

DURING THE DAY, I was sent to school, which I loathed. Over the years these establishments blurred into one; first was Saxenholme, then Trinity Hall, then my mother moved me again to St Wyburn's, all private schools housed in Victorian villas similar to the one we lived in. All had elderly teachers with bad breath and hallways that smelt of rotting cabbage and beeswax. I hated them all. Southport seemed to be full of these dull places, catering for parents whose only ambition for their daughters was that they would speak nicely and not get any big ideas. Girls were to be kept away from the riff-raff at the academically superior high school where they might become rebellious and get their ears pierced or think of going to university.

After my father's death my mother had needed to find schools where she could keep me absent for long periods. She seemed to stay under the radar for most of the time, and I got away with absences that would be unthinkable now.

These schools also had the advantage that she could more easily harass the head teacher over a matter very close to her heart: that I, Sally, was not to be involved in any kind of physical education, or to ever, ever get my hair wet.

Audrey had an intense dislike of *all* sports, or for any kind of exercise apart, of course, from dancing. She believed that swimming and having damp hair led to colds or, even worse, dull ratty hair. On the few days that I had failed to escape school altogether she would give me a note excusing me from any such exertions.

My mother had this idea that saving your energy rather than squandering it on unnecessary activity was obviously sensible. It left you plenty of zest for the important business of getting what you actually wanted, which was hardly a net-ball trophy.

My intermittent spells at one school were made more miserable by its unfortunate system of making certain girls into prefects. These chosen girls had a special sitting room with a kettle and armchairs that only they could use at break time. A further privilege offered to prefects was the use of a grassy hedged-in walkway around the top of the gardens called the Lady Walk.

The sense of being left out that I'd felt at junior school, and which echoed my mother's own social exclusion, was now perpetuated as I peered into the cosy fug of hot chocolate and chatter in the Prefect Room, only to get a smug look from those inside. Debbie Underwood of the long legs and blonde hair, the lovely parents, fun brother and holidays in Appleby, was usually to be seen handing out the biscuits in this exclusive refuge, or strolling the Lady Walk arm in arm with another popular girl.

Academically, the whole thing felt like a horrible mistake. It was a mystery to me. I felt so much cleverer than many of the girls around me, and could talk about things in a much more adult and articulate way, and yet I was quite unable to understand most of the teaching. To intensify the humiliation, a league-table list would be read aloud at the end of each term, with my name called out last, always the bottom of the class. Soon I found it impossible to stay in the school building at all.

At first I would just feign stomach ache. The stomach pains had once been a genuine complaint, almost certainly as a result of life on the road, the strange food and anxiety. I had been admitted to hospital in Liverpool for tests, which found nothing, but this condition became very useful for getting me out of the horror of these schools where I had no friends and I had missed too many classes to ever catch up.

If I protested in the morning my mother would just send away Mr Moore and his taxi. She would tell him that I was unwell again, and he would nod politely and pass on his best wishes to me before driving off.

On some days she would remember that this was breaking the law, and I would be bundled into the taxi and simply forced to go. Mr Moore would drive me there solemnly, so as to report back to my mother, and wait to see me going through the school gates. There I would hide behind a hedge until he had driven away, then slip back out to the street and walk quickly off before I was spotted by a teacher.

This lack of school could then leave a long day yawning empty ahead of me. I was out and about in Southport in all weathers in search of things to do, but it never stopped giving me a thrill of freedom. As an explorer I could go anywhere; I was no longer confined to the Prince Hotel or Marshall and Snelgrove, I now had the whole town as my territory.

There was no shortage of money, as I had what my mother and I called my 'magic purse'. I would leave this on my dressing table and it would always be stuffed with bank-notes whenever it ran low. I have no sense of how much this was, as it was unending so there was no need to count it. I simply knew that there was nothing I couldn't do or buy within the limits of our Southport world.

I used these funds for my personal 'projects' which were to do with a hazy notion of self-improvement that would somehow be far better than school. I knew I didn't want to be 'thick' but only had a vague notion of what not being 'thick' involved.

Books were not popular with my mother, despite her own gift for storytelling and her youthful success with the gossip column of the *Southport Visitor*. But reading other people's stories never interested her. She called magazines 'books' and only owned two works of fiction, a Georgette Heyer and an Agatha Christie; for some reason, although I was an obsessive reader, I never picked them up and they sat for years undisturbed on the bookshelf beside the tele-phone directory.

I hadn't yet thought of going to a library, but jumble sales yielded a wonderful and inspiringly random mix of fiction and non-fiction. It was at a jumble sale I found a pink cloth-bound book that changed my not-quite-ten-year-old life.

It had a strong musty library smell, the spine was faded and the front cover embossed with gilded roses below its title: *The Young Eve – A Weekend Book for Girls*. When I opened the pages, the paper thick and stiff, the writer immediately spoke to me in the voice of the mother that I sometimes longed for. This lady author was Julie Andrews as Maria in *The Sound of Music*, her voice warm, clear and essentially 'good', and she told me that the ideas in this book 'have you – dear lively, wide-awake young Eve of today – closely in mind . . . with your mood of looking forward into the exciting future'.

I still have it, and just the sight of its dusty pink cover brings these early years of my life flooding back. There is a deep and satisfying thrill that the chapter titles and pictures still awake in me, a reminder of how a whole new future suddenly hovered into view. It was one that I hadn't imagined was possible for me, but this book told me that it was, and gave me clear instructions on how to prepare for it.

It became my secondary education, a manual for adult life, and I followed its recommendations to the letter. These were to 'develop interests' and to greet the world with a big friendly smile 'more attractive to many people than classical beauty'.

But the most revelatory chapters were on careers and the 'fascinating array of opportunities' now open to girls. Although it had been published a year before I was born, it was positively progressive compared to the values of the strange world I shared with my mother.

Audrey had a category of poor creatures she called 'career girls' who lived pitiful solitary lives in small rented flats. They ranked below even 'domestic types' who slaved all day in a kitchen for dull husbands. The types she applauded were the 'make-the-most-of-yourself girls' and the 'tryers'; at the top of the tree were 'show girls' who tended to be statuesque with long legs, and 'glamour girls' who had just got it all right and had diamonds in their ears and great mink coats. The girls in the pages of *The Young Eve* were nothing like that, and they had dazzling careers as photographers and actresses, artists and adventurers. They may have chanced upon boy-friends along the way, boyfriends who may one day become husbands, but this didn't require them to give up these jobs so they could spend all day clothes shopping or at the hair-dresser. These girls still found time for climbing mountains and riding horses, directing plays or sailing boats to exotic islands . . . and all this in their spare time from their 'career'. It suggested you first 'master the prosaic arts of shorthand and typewriting', but said that this could lead to writ-ing 'novels or film scripts' or even 'interviewing interesting people and describing dramatic events on the radio or tele-vision' and that working in film could take you 'to the South Seas or the sewers of Paris'. How much more exciting this sounded as a reason for travel than our own desperate trek to these places.

The Young Eve's chapter, 'Dreaming of Fame', explained that 'building castles whose pinnacles touch the stars is a glorious game. It is not entirely a game either, for all the great futures began deep in the dreams of somebody.' It was permission to grow my own dreams into something real, and it told me how to go about it.

Suddenly the yawningly empty weekdays were an opportunity rather than a misery to be got through.

The affectionate voice of the lady narrator described to 'darling young Eve' the magic of theatre, and revealed to her the brilliance of Shakespeare; it explained why 'a room of one's own' was the beating heart of a creative life. There were chapters that opened new worlds of longing and would be read over and over again, such as the one about the delights of the countryside and healthy walks . . . There were so many ideas which were quite new to me but somehow felt like small golden keys that could finally open the doors to the world I really ought to be living in.

There was an interesting chapter on cordon bleu cooking which I longed to try, but we had no kitchen. First I wanted to eat it. Food at home was the cheap fried food on offer from the Back Flat. Every night I would ask the current housekeeper for the safest option, the chip butty served with a cup of sweet tea.

My mother was suspicious of food, and when travelling she would always find the simplest and most familiar British dish on the menu, usually chicken and chips, and often would just have the pudding or ice cream. I never saw her eat a vegetable or piece of fruit, although oddly she appeared to glow with health.

The next time we found ourselves in a fancy restaurant, I enquired if anything was cordon bleu. I then insisted on the waiter's suggestion, boeuf Stroganoff. She rolled her eyes to make me feel silly, and told me that I wouldn't like it and it was a waste of money.

But I clearly remember, all these years and however many thousand meals later, that very first mind-blowing taste of the rich wine sauce, with its Sixties-style dash of brandy and double cream. New worlds opened up to me as I scooped up the plump rice, buttery mushrooms and tender shreds of beef.

She was wrong, and yet again *The Young Eve* was right! I had wasted years of hotel dining rooms by avoiding things with fancy names. Suddenly menus became wondrous things that I would pore over, with such gorgeous names as 'crêpes Suzette', 'chicken Kiev' and 'poires belle Hélène'. From that day I would enter restaurants with excitement, breathing in the decadent smells in the air, feeling a thrill as the menus were handed to us.

Once we were back in Southport I became determined to find these amazing dishes for myself. Where in Southport, on a weekday lunchtime, could a runaway schoolgirl go to find this food?

I must have wandered the streets sniffing. I found one small café, in a back street leading down to the seafront, where I caught the scents of garlic and wine seeping out of an extractor fan, drifting on the sea breeze as I passed. It was a reassuringly simple place with Formica tables and plastic squeezy tomatoes of sauce, but in the glass cabinet, alongside the limp egg sandwiches, was a tray of home-made lasagne, glistening with its oven-baked creamy golden topping, rich meat juices oozing at the edges.

The Italian owner and his wife watched me with looks of amusement as I ate with gusto. I was hooked and soon I was in there most lunchtimes. My schooldays developed a new pattern: delivered by Mr Moore and his taxi to the school gate, I would wait impatiently through morning prayers and the first couple of meaningless lessons. Then, released by the mid-morning break, I would run out the back gates behind the netball courts and down to the seafront to bide my time till lunch.

My book propped open against a plastic tomato, I would settle in as the promising vapours from the kitchen intensified and then lunch was ready. I revelled in the ritual of the delicious food and the feeling of comfort.

Becoming braver, I ventured to Chez Nico, a cosy place with candles in Chianti bottles encased in woven raffia on red gingham tablecloths, and a bar decorated with hanging plastic vegetables. A dish called pilaf with prawns and peppers arrived in front of me, the waiter giving me a long glance as he placed the plate on the table.

Occasionally, I sat near a solitary local businessman or office worker, and they would ask about the book I happened to be reading at the time. I thought it clever if I could describe the storyline in just a couple of sentences. If anyone ever asked whether my parents were nearby, I was always ready with: 'I just had a doctor's appointment, and my mum has just dropped me off while she does some shopping.' I felt free, out of the wind and rain, and with a feeling that now I could think and plan the rest of my life.

19

Crashing into Gateposts

It was a warm evening in late summer and my mother was going mad with frustration, pacing the landing between her bedroom and the bathroom. She was putting on her lipstick, frowning in the mirror and then wiping it off again. Through the open window was the drone of traffic, as cars full of families headed home from a day at the seaside along the main road. I sat curled up in the chair in her pink, perfumed bedroom, trying to read my book but feeling horribly infected by her restless mood. This atmosphere had been hanging heavily over us for much of the summer. I knew it well, and that it only vanished when the suitcases were open on the bed and we were about to go travelling, or, as she would say, 'Let's get out of this bloody town and get this show on the road!'

But I can't do it again. I know I can't survive another pointless trip to the other side of the world and back. I can't survive weeks in a hotel room with windows that won't open, waiting for the signal that we are finally moving on because the mission has once again failed.

The house seemed less and less like a home. These silent musty antique-filled rooms felt like the stage set for a play that never happened. Audrey had retreated to her bedroom where she created another, very different world, one that felt like her true self: bright, modern and scented.

She still loved her car, though, and the thrill of roaring off away from the house, the town, her problems and the depth of her gloom, even when she didn't have anywhere to go. I knew that some nights, in a panic at the quiet house, she would drive out to the motorway service station after midnight. She had told me, 'It's the only place that's open all night, and, you know, there are people there.'

That evening she took me out with her, holding open the passenger door impatiently: 'Come on, Miss Flip, quickety hop.' Although I was growing up she still talked to me in our special language, a mix of song, baby talk and euphemism.

The car was still hot from the sunny day and my legs stuck to the pale blue leather upholstery. 'Can we open the sunshine roof?' I begged, as sometimes she let me stand on the passenger seat with my head sticking out of the roof while she drove. She even let me drive on the beach sometimes, in big circles going from the sand dunes out to the distant sea. But that time she just shook her head, the air between us thick with warm, salty intent.

We drove in a rare silence. Usually she sang and always something which was perfect for the moment. This was a game we played, to find the right song for every occasion. Certain things, such as a hazy moon, the mention of Paris, the sight of a fallen rose . . . these were likely to set off a full-blown medley. But even starting up the car to go to the corner shop would at least warrant a short burst of some long-forgotten music-hall repertoire:

> We're off, we're off,
> we're off in our motorcar.
> There's sixty bobbies after us
> and we don't know where we are.

Some of these songs were a remnant from her time as a little Tapper in a Topper on the stage of the Liverpool Empire; others were from the crooners that she loved and were about solid-gold Cadillacs or cars with weird American names.

> Come away with me, Sally,
> in my merry Oldsmobile,
> down the road of life we'll fly,
> automobubbling, you and I . . .

Now it was the Sixties and she was on a drive to catch up with the times, flicking her hair up at the ends and squeezing into Tricel bell-bottoms in psychedelic colours. The record player by her dressing table no longer played her beloved Nat King Cole, but had been usurped by a transistor, tuned to Radio Caroline. That summer the open windows of Bluebird poured out the Beatles songs she had learnt.

'*Baby, you can drive my car . . . doo, doo, doo . . .*'

Mr Buttress, our neighbour, said to me, 'Your mother is very with it!'

'Where are we going?' I knew that this sudden decisive mood was not just about fish and chips, or popping in to Auntie Ava's for a coffee.

'Out!' She didn't want to tell me, and I could sense that ruthless determination that rose up in her so quickly, and fuelled so much that we did.

'You'll see,' she snapped when I pressed her.

We drove, heading out of town a few miles, past the golf club, and then turned into a wide residential street, tree-lined. She stopped the car, switched off the engine. We sat in silence. I listened to the hot metal ticking quietly, the windows were down, and birdsong drifted in. I stared out at the big detached houses set back among leafy gardens and asked, 'Why are we here?'

She shushed me.

She was staring at the house opposite. Behind a pair of tall wrought-iron gates hung from sandstone posts, a gravel drive arced up to a red-bricked Edwardian villa half hidden behind linden trees. I could see the tail end of a large car parked by the house and a recently used lawn mower beside it.

Nothing happened. The engine ticked, the birds sang.

'What are we doing?' I complained, sighing theatrically.

She frowned. 'Shh!' I could hear her thinking, brain clicking away, like a cat figuring out how to strike its prey.

Suddenly her jaw tightened, she touched her hair and started the engine. We shot forward a few yards, she skidded to a stop, threw the car in reverse and roared backwards, swinging the steering wheel.

'Mummy!'

I was screaming as the rear of the car bumped up over the pavement and smashed into the stone gatepost with a bang.

'Why did you do that?' I screeched, furious. 'You did that on purpose!'

'Not a word!' She calmly switched off the engine again, checked her lipstick in the mirror, climbed out, walked around the front of the car to open my door, took my arm and pulled me. Then we walked up the driveway, past the parked car and lawn mower, and were standing at the front door, Audrey ringing the bell insistently.

She gave me a look that told me that she was not to be messed with. The door opened and a man stood there. He was tall, his grey hair receding and his cardigan oddly scruffy.

He looked stony, as if he didn't want anyone to ring his doorbell.

'I am so sorry,' she said sweetly, instantly transforming herself into someone rather fragile. 'I've just had the most terrible accident. I was trying to turn around and I seem to have driven into your gatepost.'

I couldn't tell if he was going to be cross or not. He came out and walked to the bottom of the drive. He looked at the gatepost, and the crumpled back of our car.

'I'll get a pen and paper, and my insurance details,' he said, and was about to go back into the house, but she was too quick for him.

'Could you possibly get me a glass of water?' she asked. 'I'm feeling a little faint.'

'Oh, yes . . . erm, yes of course.'

As he turned away to get the water, she struck again.

'I'm so sorry to ask, but is there anywhere I could sit down, just for a moment?' she said, putting her hand to her throat, and adding a perfectly pitched tremble to her voice.

He hesitated. I could see that he very much didn't want to have us in his house, but couldn't think of an excuse. He held the door open for us to go in.

The kitchen was large and new, but bare, unused-looking. There was a plate with a half-finished meal on the table. He was eating his dinner when we so rudely, deliberately, interrupted. The table was just set for one, and then it clicked. I suddenly realized why we were there.

She had done her research and swung the operation into gear with precision. Peter Aspinall was a widower, with a teenage son away at boarding school. His wife had died of cancer soon after their son, Keith, was born and Peter had found it difficult to recover from the loss. He had done well in business, working his way up to become managing director of a small sweet factory that made the bright pink sticks of rock sold down on the seafront with the word 'Southport' running through the middle of them. He had expanded the firm's lines of sweets, won some lucrative export contracts abroad and made some money. None of this was obvious from the rather empty and lifeless house.

I later discovered that for some years Peter had been unsuccessfully targeted as a potential love interest for the single women of Southport. Married couples would persistently invite him to dinner parties, where he would be introduced to their single lady friend. His golf partners, pushed by their wives into insisting that he join them for golf-club dinner dances, would then give him faintly apologetic looks as he arrived to find an unattached divorcée there to make up a foursome. He eventually stopped going out at all, and became something of a recluse.

My mother had heard these stories, and realized that the only way to meet him was a more direct ambush. Now that we were sitting awkwardly in his kitchen, on the hard upright chairs with our glasses of water, I was wondering if she was regretting it. Peter seemed so sombre, and not remotely her type. He looked at her unhappily as she prattled on, trying to make any sort of connection.

'Oh, is that from Switzerland, a real cow bell?' She had alighted on the only decorative object in the room. 'I'd love to go to Switzerland, the air must be so clean.'

He was holding the piece of paper with his insurance details on it, as if expecting us to leave.

She sipped her water. 'We've travelled a lot, Sally and I, it's been quite an education for her. Gosh, we've had some adventures, haven't we, poppet?'

I gave the faintest nod. I wasn't going to help her out this time.

Even she could not spin things out any longer, and we were soon back at the front door, having checked that our car was probably all right to be driven to the garage. There was a shaking of hands, phone numbers exchanged, and we all said our goodbyes, agreeing that the gatepost be discussed at a later date.

Her mood was giving nothing away as we drove off, and I didn't speak either, feeling that the obvious failure of the expedition was punishment enough for her having behaved so badly. She didn't seem too despondent and I grudgingly admired the way that she had pulled it off.

She would often say that 'all the world loves a tryer' and it was true for me; I mostly liked to see her trying and would have been sorry to see her give up.

I was amazed when, a week or so later, she announced that she was going out for dinner with the gatepost man. Soon after that he appeared again, to take her for lunch at a country restaurant near Formby, and they wanted me to come. My mother did much of the talking, but he tried to engage me, asking me questions about school without realizing this was the last topic I'd be interested in.

'What is your favourite subject, Sally? Your geography must be up to scratch with all this travelling you and your mother have done?'

'She's not too keen on school,' my mother laughed. 'She's been spoilt – too much fun outside school to settle down to a routine.'

My mother was working harder than I had ever seen her, and I was mystified as to why, when he seemed so quiet and ordinary. I had heard her say 'any old port in a storm', but surely this was more like shipwreck on a completely deserted beach. It was hard to believe that after all our long search she was now chasing this poor man who simply happened to live up the road and be alone.

20

Further Afield

SINCE THE GATEPOST INCIDENT, my mother had been in a strange and withdrawn state. She drove past Peter Aspinall's house each night peering at the windows, and she and Auntie Ava had long whispered conversations that I struggled to overhear. Ava called him 'your Southport Rock Magnate' and didn't seem as enthusiastic about him as she had been about my mother's other possibilities.

The whole thing worried me, but at least it left me free to follow my new obsession, which was doing as many things as possible that were recommended by *The Young Eve*. The desperate behaviour of my mother seemed more bizarre than ever, and now that I had this other calm, clear voice to guide me I wanted to follow it in every way I could. It terrified me to think that another travel plan of my mother's could interrupt my precious project.

One chapter in my bible described the uplifting effect of a theatre visit and I'd seen a poster for a play at the local Little Theatre. As I was taking so many days off school it was exciting to find a new place to spend cold or wet afternoons – a midweek matinee.

The following Wednesday afternoon I sat, delighted, among the pensioners and watched a musical called *The Boyfriend*. I was already something of an expert on film musicals, as my mother had an endless repertoire and I could have performed most of the well-known ones, from *Gigi* to *The Gay Divorcee*, tunelessly but practically word-perfect.

But the real live thing, up there on a stage, amazed me: those lights, those sets and costumes that appeared at first glance to be so clunky and fake, and yet managed to convince us so completely of these other worlds – the whole effect felt like the closest I had come to witnessing magic. It also felt like where I wanted to be, more than anywhere. From a wet autumn afternoon I had stepped into this cosy, plush, red-velvet murmur, waited for the curtain to go up and the lights to dim, and felt completely at home.

There was a friendly lady in the box office, and I made enquiries.

'Well, there's the Playhouse in Liverpool; they do marvellous things.'

Liverpool was twenty miles away but the pull was strong. So it was a Wednesday morning when I stepped up onto the train and sat counting off the numerous stations en route to the city as the low flat landscape scrolled by. Many of these places where we squeaked to a halt had featured in our life, and were places with a story. This somehow made the journey feel further, as though I was somehow travelling back on this adventure through my own past.

Here was Birkdale, home of the Royal Golf Club where my mother longed to be accepted and never was. It often hosted the famous Ryder Cup, which drew the rich and famous to Southport, and its exclusive clubhouse held dinner dances throughout the year. Even though my mother liked to call it fuddy-duddy, it pained her that she could not be part of its upmarket, snobby social life. I heard her tell Auntie Ava that 'it didn't take Jewish members either' and wondered what the 'either' meant.

Birkdale had sand dunes, and Southport's only hill where people, though not me, would go tobogganing if there was snow.

Then there came Ainsdale, where I could see the Sands, a nightclub that my mother would often go to.

Formby had the richest history for us. It was where James, the real love of my mother's life, lived with his wife and children. Then on to the unknown and unknowable Hightown and Hall Road to Blundell Sands and Crosby.

Crosby was very familiar, being the home of Auntie Grace and Uncle Phil, so it was strange to pass it, alone on the train, and see the Angel War Memorial and think that just beyond it was the small house with the horse brasses around the fireplace and pampas grasses on the hall landing.

Mainly I loved travelling past all these landmarks of my childhood and feeling them change into something quite new. Now they were part of a journey I was on alone, and that somehow transformed them. I thought that one day I might find myself in some of those strange and distant places

I'd visited with my mother, and they too would be almost unrecognizable.

Arriving in Liverpool, I felt like I had travelled to New York. Even on days out there with my mother it seemed huge and exotic. We would go to the Adelphi Hotel's Zodiac Coffee Bar for toasted sandwiches, a place we loved as it was done out in a funky Sixties style and the waitress would ask what sign you were born under, and then give you the right menu. Mummy made her laugh by saying, 'Me! I was born under a warning sign!' We'd sit there and make up silly astrological fortunes for each other. 'An unusual situation today has left you speechless . . .' she'd begin, then she put her finger to her coral lips. And we'd both sit in silence until I finally 'get it' and we both collapse in giggles.

We had once been to the Cavern Club to see the Beatles play, and my mother had held me up and danced with me in her arms, but I was too little to remember it now and it had just become a story. Although London was the ultimate thrill, Liverpool was grand enough to feel like a big city, with its vast buildings coated in the velvety blackness of the centuries and the contrasting ranks of windows catching the low sunlight.

When the train arrived at Exchange Station, with a jolt and a hiss, I experienced a wave of panic. Navigating the vaguely familiar streets to the Playhouse Theatre, the trip felt the bravest thing I had ever done; but at last I was here, and only had to deal with the box office and dodge the usual questions about the whereabouts of my mother. 'She's just dropped me off. She's gone shopping and is going to pick me up at the end.' At last I held that magic ticket and I entered the longed-for darkness and pools of illumination.

The play was extraordinary. The story was very odd indeed, and yet an audience had paid money to come, and were sitting in rapt attention.

But why? Why did everyone keep talking about a wild duck? As this was the title of the play, it obviously wasn't just a minor detail but something important to the story.

I discussed this with a lady who worked at the theatre. She couldn't help me with the wild-duck issue, but she said that the next production might be more suitable for me and she gave me a leaflet. She was right, and I then became a regular.

The haunting Irish cadences of *Playboy of the Western World* were the sounds of somewhere half familiar to me, as if from a dream; the strangeness of Shakespeare's couples in *As You Like It*, sticking notes on trees in a forest, speaking that rich poetic language which hinted at some important truths that would be mine if it could only be decoded. These words were spoken by people with Sandie Shaw or Paul McCartney haircuts, and wearing miniskirts and bell-bottoms; strobe lights flashed and pop music played, all of which made the archaic language seem even more mystifying.

I remember that this thing called 'history' suddenly made sense. I saw Greek tragedy played by actors in US army uniforms set against a backdrop of the Vietnam War and Kennedy's assassination. I saw a Restoration play done with full Hogarthian filth, in dirty costumes and among stinking rubbish as the actors fought and spat their way through the story; and I had the first glimmering that the past is 'another country' far more strange than most of the places my mother's travels had taken us to.

I would learn many years later that I had in fact chanced on something genuinely amazing. As it happened, these Liverpool theatres, a half-hour train ride from my home, were going through a famously golden era, and at ten or eleven years old I was able to watch actors like Anthony Hopkins, Judi Dench and Ian McKellan perform in experimental work that was getting incredible national reviews.

I felt proud that I'd discovered this phenomenon. The Playhouse had queues around the block, even for the mati- nee. So I had stumbled upon something that really was as wondrous as it seemed and these crowds of people agreed with me.

My mother had missed all this, but I'd found it for myself.

It was around this time of stalking the poor gatepost man that I began to suspect Audrey was regretting the fact I was growing up. When I was younger it had seemed like all she wanted was for me to become an adult, but now she was realizing that this meant I was finding new things of my own and I might not accept her wisdom on absolutely everything. I knew she was hugely missing our double act.

She still wanted me to curl up on the bed as I used to and she would pat the covers as if I were a small cat.

'Come and be a snuggle pie and tell me what you've been up to.'

'Not much,' I would say. 'Reading, mostly.'

I didn't want her to mock any of my new discoveries, so I secretly hugged them to myself. I realized that I desperately wanted the gatepost man to take care of her now, but there were so many things that could still go wrong.

I wasn't sure how much Peter had worked out about my mother's ways of making money. I knew that she was terrified of admitting to the betting shops.

Even Ava, hardly my mother's most astute critic, had spotted trouble. 'You probably should tell the Rock Magnate a few things, you know?' she said cautiously.

Peter had told my mother quite early on how much he loathed gambling of any kind, and that he particularly hated the place opposite the gates of his own factory, a squalid betting shop where he would see the poor workers go in with their hard-earned pay packets and come out crushed and defeated.

'There aren't even supposed to be places like this on residential streets,' he said, shaking his head, 'so there has obviously been some sort of corruption going on.'

This was particularly tricky for my mother, because the shop in question was one of her own, and permission for it had been bought with those clinking bottles of champagne in the boot of our car, as well as who-knows-what other 'favours'. Peter had failed to notice that the sign above Miller's Betting Shop was my mother's own maiden name.

She was finally forced to confess, and he was appalled. He tried to find excuses for her – that she was a single woman, desperate, and with a child to support – and she eagerly went along with any exonerating suggestions he came up with.

He seemed very upset. She said she would change over the betting shops to hair salons, and was soon busy replacing the seedy chain-smoking managers with pretty receptionists and hair stylists. With this more respectable business to her name, he began to calm down but would at times give her a look that he hadn't given her before. It was either sadness or suspicion.

I realized that if Peter was so shocked by her lack of morality, then things were a little worse than I'd thought. In the light of this, her other sources of income were much more worrying. How would he react to the news about her 'girls' and the 'dates' she arranged and the fact that she was so notorious in the town?

During one of the rather heated discussions about the betting shops, Peter had mentioned something called a 'moral compass', and I wasn't sure that we had one. I panicked. Their relationship was now looking like a possible lifesaver for us both, but it clearly could flounder if certain things came to light.

My fears led me to my latest interest, which was an exploration of religion and morality. I'd imagined a voice in my head, rather like that of *The Young Eve*, but this new voice would be able to tell me what was right and wrong, or good and bad. Perhaps some more 'goodness' in our life might also dispel the slightly 'off' smell that seemed to hang around us.

My mother thought I was a crashing bore when I talked about any of this and loathed anything to do with mysticism or religion. We lived a few houses along from St James's, an ugly red-stone Victorian church presided over by the eager figure of Canon Jones. He was enormously tall and looked like Plug from 'The Bash Street Kids'. He must have known that our household was in need of spiritual and moral guidance, given my father's death and my mother's deteriorating reputation over the years. He had been quite persistent in his visits and would come loping up our drive in his black cassock with bony ankles showing beneath, his beaming face full of a desire to save us.

My mother would peer out, groan, 'Oh no! It's Canon Jones,' and hide behind the curtains.

One day, when she was out, I rebelled and let him into the house. We had an interesting chat about good and evil, but I found his views a little on the dull side, to the relief of my mother.

Then I found something more intriguing. There was a week when I didn't even pretend to go to school. Each day I walked into town and sat in the El Cabala coffee bar reading my book until the Odeon opened for its matinee showing of *On a Clear Day You Can See Forever*.

Settling in, the lights went down and there she was again, Barbra Streisand in this bizarre, unfathomable tale of Daisy Gamble who has strange mind-reading powers. She undergoes hypnosis to stop smoking, but then finds she has gone back to her previous incarnation as Lady Melinda Tentrees, an eighteenth-century English aristocrat who parades around Brighton Pavilion in fabulous Cecil Beaton costumes.

In the film's interval one afternoon, I ate my ice cream and noticed a man sitting near me in the auditorium. He had a rather unkempt beard but a kindly face, so I asked him what he thought of the film. Had he worked out why Daisy kept turning into Lady Melinda?

He then explained the principle of reincarnation and I asked him what he thought about this idea. He said that he wasn't a believer himself, but imagined people might believe in it because they felt there were other selves inside them they couldn't explain, though these were more likely to come from their parents than past lives, in his view. It was a really interesting conversation and I wondered if this was why I felt that there were different selves inside of me, all wanting to be the real me. Did they come from my father, or had I been someone in another life?

He then told me that reincarnation was popular in India. India! I had been taken with India since I had first heard its name, conjuring fantasies of spices and yellow sunlight and desert palaces.

My mother had no interest in going to India, despite my pleas. She said it wasn't 'us', which suddenly made it more appealing.

'It might be me, but not you!' I said and she looked hurt at this, so I didn't say any more.

I'd seen a poster of an Indian man down by Pleasure-land, the fairground, with an arrow pointing to a brightly painted kiosk covered with images of crystal balls and stars. I followed the arrows and inside there was a small dark man seated on a cushion, wearing a colourful waistcoat and saffron turban. Joss sticks burnt in a holder, and pictures of temples had been stuck to the walls. The man asked me to sit across from him, then he looked at my palm and face for a time. His eyes were almost closed and I wondered if he had fallen asleep.

'Yes,' he said, as if inviting a question.

'I wanted to know if I have different selves in me, and which is the right one?' Then I quickly added, 'Oh, and what my future holds.'

Finally he spoke in a heavy accent. 'You can only seek the true self within.' He opened his eyes. 'And one day you will visit India, my country, and also many, many other places. I see you in a big shiny car, in a big city, very successful.'

This was just what I wanted to hear, and gave a kind of weird blessing to my growing ideas of reinvention. So it felt like a magical prophesy already coming to pass when, one wintry day some months later, India seemed to be coming to me. The gloom of our wide road lit up with the headlights of a removal van followed by two Rolls-Royces, and from these emerged a chattering flock of brilliant creatures, with slivers of neon-coloured saris wafting out from under flapping mackintoshes.

These women in their gorgeous clothes would emerge from the Victorian porch of the house next door, jangling forth with their arms laden with bangles to strew the house with fairy lights, even though Christmas had long since passed. There were wonderful smells and sounds escaping from the leaded-light windows. There was also a discreet sign in the driveway, inviting visitors to their Sunday-evening puja or religious celebration. There were few Indians in Southport, and Dr Naidoo had bought the next-door house for both his vast extended family and as a place of local worship. Perhaps this was what I was looking for.

My mother now perked up at the idea of me trying out the Naidoos' puja; it was entertaining and promised the added pleasure of finding out exactly what went on next door. I had also pointed out that the Beatles, who she loved, were in India and doing just this kind of thing. I begged her to come but she just said, 'Well you can pray for me, but I'm probably a lost cause!'

Sunday evening, and the Naidoos' living room was filled with chairs in front of a shrine. There were pictures of crazy looking gods and set before these was a silver tray covered in incense burners smouldering their sweet smell into the room, and surrounded by bells, fruit, flowers and cups full of rainbow powders. There was a special armchair draped in a white sheet for the Master. Someone explained to me that his physical being wouldn't be present, just his spirit. There was a bottom-shaped dent in the sheet that I assumed was made by the Master sitting there.

We sang songs; one I remember was about walking through life 'with my Master by my side' and when I sang it to my mother she laughed.

'That's a Scottish song and they've just changed the words' and she sang: *'Roamin' in the gloamin' wi' ma lassie by ma side . . .'*

I feared she would kill the magic if I told her any more. So I decided to keep the Sunday evenings to myself and practise my meditation and the search for my 'Third Eye' in the privacy of my bedroom.

My mother always seemed amazed that I was interested in things that she thought 'a bore' and, having mentioned my father very little, his name now came up more often as she would tell people, 'She's just like Neil,' if I seemed to take anything too seriously or challenged her view of the world.

Perhaps I wanted to be like Neil; I knew I wanted to be something that wasn't quite her. I'd recently watched *A Streetcar Named Desire* with awful glimpses of recognition, and was now haunted by a sense of how my mother's Scarlett O'Hara could morph into Blanche DuBois in an instant, relying too much on 'the kindness of strangers' who might not always be kind. I wondered what would become of her if Peter didn't take her on, and where we would be now if he had not opened his front door that day. He seemed like her only chance, and I hoped she was not going to mess it up. After all every man in our life so far had bolted or been rejected, so what would go wrong this time?

21

High Hopes

It felt like the middle of the night when I woke up, and I immediately thought that something must be wrong. My mother had been out for dinner with Peter, and now here she was, sitting on the edge of my bed, something she would not usually do. She told me quietly that she had some news: Peter had proposed to her. I said something like, 'That's nice,' then she kissed me and crept out again, leaving me bemused.

At that moment, and for the following weeks, I had no idea what she really thought about this. She seemed to be in a trance, and it was hard to know if it was a happy trance or an unhappy one. Although she had gone after him in the most direct way possible, it had been almost a reflex action with no consideration for the consequences.

The success of the mission had left her, for once, speechless. Suddenly she was wearing an engagement ring that she kept staring at as if she couldn't believe it was real. I recalled, with some fear, the catastrophic effect of Bathsheba's Valentine provocation in *Far from the Madding Crowd*, aimed at getting the attention of poor reclusive Mr Boldwood. Would Peter now be driven mad like Mr Boldwood, and shoot people if she didn't follow through and accept him? Was Peter Cooper her Sergeant Troy who would arrive on the eve of the wedding and cause disaster?

Peter Aspinall wasn't the fun stepfather I had hoped for, like Ronnie Carroll or Mick the wrestler. He wasn't deliciously charming like Peter Cooper or Sabet Sabescue. But I sensed that he was kind and he really loved her, and I now felt terribly sorry for him. I remembered Humphrey's sigh of 'Divine Discontent' as he watched her wandering that cruise ship on her eternal search, and wondered if it meant that she would always be discontented, and if so how would poor Peter manage?

My own life changed little. Peter would pick her up to go out for dinner at a time when I was, as usual, in the Back Flat or in my room, so I didn't see much of him. Usually he behaved as if he wanted to be friendly to me, but wasn't sure what to say to a young girl. He probably assumed that I went to school, had some friends, and lived a more normal life than I actually did. I suspected that he knew very little about my mother and was about to have a series of shocks.

The wedding they were planning seemed rather low-key and unromantic and my mother's trance continued. It was to be a winter wedding, and I was to wear a red velvet dress with a fur hat and muff. I didn't understand why they were waiting so long when they could have had a lovely summer wedding, and I was sure that my mother was having second thoughts. Possibly Peter was too, though for different reasons. They both acted a little awkwardly with each other, and this was something I had never seen before where my mother was concerned.

To my huge relief the big gloomy house where I had been so unhappy was now sold to developers, to be turned into a vast nursing home. Peter was selling his villa and we were all going to move into a bright, sunny detached house that was being redecorated. It had a large garden backing onto the sand dunes with a gate onto the beach. It was a short stroll to the golf course, which Peter loved. The house was perfect, almost like the American suburban house in *Bewitched*.

It was almost beyond perfect, having a lower-ground 'party room' facing onto the garden. This was decorated with lush murals of South Sea Island girls and palm trees, all done by the artist who was responsible for the exuberant paintings that adorned my beloved Pleasureland, as if this room had actually been created with me in mind.

Above all, to my mother's consternation, there was a big American-style kitchen with an alcove with a table and chairs. My mother's trance may have been fear of discovery of her wicked past, but it was possibly more about now having to produce a meal. She had been avoiding the discussion up to this point, steering Peter towards meals out and never offering anything at home.

My mother and I were moving into the new house that summer, and then Peter would move in with his son Keith after the wedding. Keith, my teenage now-to-be stepbrother, had hardly spoken to me and turned red whenever I spoke to him. He was still away at boarding school and my mother and Peter seemed to be worried about his reaction to the sudden change in his father's life. They wanted him to get used to the idea over the summer, before the wedding. We'd had one rather stilted meal out together when Keith had shyly presented me with a bear that banged a drum, which I was told had been a favourite toy, and I recognized that this was a sign that he hoped for my friendship.

My fears that something would go terribly wrong were gradually subsiding, but there was one difficult conversation about a possible 'house-warming party'. Peter said that he hadn't yet met any of my mother's friends, and as she had insisted the wedding group be so small, he suggested that this might be a nice opportunity.

There was a pause in the conversation, a moment of silence, when my mother didn't know what to say. I imagined her going through the potential guest list in her mind – Auntie Ava and Uncle Anthony, Auntie Grace and Uncle Phil, perhaps some of the salesmen from Man to Man or Peter Cooper? It wouldn't be a very good party. Even Anthony was possibly off the list as my mother was upset with him. Ava was to be a maid of honour at the wedding, but Anthony didn't like the idea, and had told my mother that she should 'just get on with the whole thing quietly, before anyone has reason to change their minds'. I thought Anthony was suggesting that Peter might change his mind.

The whole question of the house-warming was difficult, as it raised other difficulties as to why we didn't seem to have any nice friends. I found myself once again looking at my red velvet dress and wondering if it would actually be worn. Far more alarming was the thought of what the rest of our life would look like if something went wrong.

Then, miraculously, a solution presented itself. My friend Jane, who lived up the road, was keen to help with a school charity fundraiser for the League of Pity. Their leaflet suggested various activities, and among them was to hold a garden party and invite neighbours and local people. This would be perfect: we could combine the house-warming with a garden party, and it was in a good cause, which would show my mother in the best possible light.

Peter would definitely see her as being normal and even generous, and be more likely to overlook any rumours he might hear and still marry her.

Jane seemed very excited and said she longed to be a Rose Queen, as she had seen one once at a fete. We began to plan the events, and were wondering who should open the party, as the leaflet suggested that a local celebrity or the mayor could be a big draw. I asked my mother about this and she said that she and the mayor weren't on good terms – something to do with her shops. She couldn't think of a celebrity either, and didn't seem interested in the garden party in the slightest, much to my annoyance given that it was all for her.

One day, at the start of the summer holidays, just after my mother and I had moved into the new house, Peter came around and was looking at furniture catalogues and I heard my mother reading something out from the *Southport Visitor*.

'Tony Tenser is about to shoot a film up the road, it says here.' She held up the page, with a photograph of him, hair

slicked back like someone who would hang around with the Rat Pack in Las Vegas.

Peter looked up.

'You know,' she said, 'he's that film producer, a bit Flash Harry. He lives in that big modern house up by Rotten Row. They're going to be filming it at the old Palace Hotel.'

The hotel where she was once a hostess to the American Air Force men had in recent years been closed down and boarded up. I was terribly excited by this news, as I was interested in films and it also struck me that perhaps Tony Tenser could open the garden party. I held back from mentioning this in case it didn't work out, instead saying that I must meet him, as 'film director' was on my career list and perhaps he would give me a job helping out on set.

'You don't want a job, don't be silly, you are too young, and what for?' she asked crossly.

'What kind of films does he make?' Peter enquired.

'All kinds, he's famous for inventing the label of "sex kitten" for Brigitte Bardot. It made her name,' my mother said with admiration.

Peter frowned, and said that he wasn't sure I should be meeting him.

'He used to do films that were a bit naughty and nudie, but he's doing arty ones now,' she reassured him. 'The one he's just produced, *Repulsion* with Roman Polanski, it sounds very arty.'

I was obsessed with meeting him now; I loved arty.

Audrey loved to fix things, so she drove me to a big house near the seafront and then she waited while I went up to the door to ask Tony Tenser if I could watch the filming. I froze, realizing I was far too shy to meet him, or even to ring his doorbell, let alone ask such a thing.

This didn't go down well.

'You'll never get anywhere in life with that attitude. You just have to march up to doors and knock on them very hard. Or give them a great big push!'

I looked blank. 'But what will I say?'

'You tell him: "I'm Sally and I'm a great admirer of yours."'

'I don't know him. I've never even seen one of his films,' I protested.

'That doesn't matter. Flattery will get you everywhere! If he wants to believe it, he will.'

'Then what?'

'Then you say, "All I want in the world is to be a film director. It's my greatest dream and passion."'

'I can't say that; it sounds silly.' I pulled a face.

'No such word as can't.' This was one of her most annoying sayings. She would always trot it out if I ever dared to admit that I couldn't do something. Her next most annoying saying was 'Don't ask, don't get'. It was that stupid ant in the 'High Hopes' song she always sang, where the little ant tries to move the rubber-tree plant. He had high hopes, she would tell me, and look what happened: he darned well moved that rubber tree.

Here it came . . . 'Don't ask, don't get! You wanted to come. I've brought you, so get on with it. Just say, "Please may I come and watch the film-making process." That's what you want, isn't it?'

I was still frozen, so she tried her Wicked Witch of the West act. She threw open the car door and screamed at me, 'Get out of this bloody car and do it! Now!'

This always shook me into action. Nothing was ever as scary as she was when she looked this way, her eyes flashing and a mean look on her face. I would rather have faced a firing squad or performed my own show at the Palladium than disobey her in this mood.

So I plucked up the courage, and marched up the driveway. I had chosen my clothes with care and was wearing my latest outfit: a red suede miniskirt with a matching jacket with a long suede fringe like a cowgirl. I had applied a lot of eyeliner in the hope that I looked much older. My mother had told me to do this in the car so that Peter wouldn't see.

Tony Tenser came to the door wearing a towelling robe and said, 'I was just tanning.' He looked rather hot and had a lot of yellowy-white hair and a moustache.

I stammered out, 'Hello, I'm Sally. I'm sorry to intrude but could I possibly talk to you for a moment?'

This would be too polite to my mother's way of thinking, but felt more 'me'. *The Young Eve* would have approved.

He asked me in, and although my mother had told me not to go inside, I couldn't resist. The house was very 'with it', with a hanging-basket chair thing on a chain, and everything – the furniture, walls and carpet – was white. It looked exactly how I imagined a film producer's house should look.

He regarded me expectantly and I launched in.

'I'm very keen to be a film director one day; it's something I feel passionately about. So, I wondered if I could possibly come and watch you at work – or perhaps help in some way?'

I had got it over with now. She wouldn't be angry. Now I just wanted to get back to the car.

Tony took a pad of paper and wrote down my name and phone number. He then looked at me and asked if I would like to actually be in the film, not a speaking role but a few shots here and there? I could hardly speak, I was so excited at the idea, and I left having got a role as an extra for the summer, for which I would be paid thirteen pounds a week.

I skipped down the drive singing about the ant and another rubber-tree plant that bites the dust.

'There you are. I told you!' she said when I climbed back into the car. She was pleased with me. I'd got what I wanted and more; maybe I was finally shaping up into something.

My preparation for the job involved trying to find outfits in which I would look older. Every Saturday I scoured the *Southport Visitor* for church-hall jumble sales and I was amassing a large wardrobe. My mother always said 'dress for the role you aspire to', so I worked on finding the right clothes for my future life, as if this might somehow make it happen. Our neighbour, Bill Tidy, a cartoonist famous in the north for his 'Cloggies' series in *Private Eye*, had once given me a lift from the bus stop to a church hall. We seemed to be friends, despite twenty years' age difference and based mainly on me standing forlornly at bus stops when he drove by. Bill had laughed at my desperation to be first at the sale, and sat watching from his car as I joined the queue waiting to

burst through the doors. He later put a drawing through the letter box of me, young and determined, long red hair flying, elbows sharpened, among the sea of old ladies. He titled it *The Seasoned Jumbler.*

There was the thrill of running first to the table of dresses and fur coats with their lovely fusty attic smell. I had already found a treasure trove of flowered dresses from the Thirties, and of Lauren Bacall-style suits with pencil skirts from the Forties. This perfect little taupe suit was for when I was a journalist, inspired by films like *The Front Page.* This tropical sundress would be ideal if I was in the Florida Keys or in Africa as a travel writer, and here was a black cocktail dress with tiny pearl buttons for nights out in Paris or at a cabaret in Berlin while my films were premiering at festivals there. Now, for my movie debut, I chose outfits that made me look as much like a hippy as possible, as I knew the film had hippies in it.

My mother seemed annoyed that my involvement with the film now involved paid work. She could see the attraction of my spending a few hours watching people work on a movie set, but was upset that this had turned into a job.

'Why do you want to get up so horribly early, and then be out all day, and maybe in the rain, maybe even getting your hair wet . . . !'

She went on and on, finding more and more objections.

The idea was an affront to her, particularly as my magic purse continued to supply all the money I could possibly want. But I was beginning to see the magic purse as something slightly sinister. It sat there on the dressing table secretly fattening itself up each day, until it was grotesquely bulging with cash: a shameful talisman of her control.

The filming day did begin horribly early. It was soon after sunrise that I rode my bicycle down to the Palace Hotel in lovely summer light. I still remember the sense of freedom from the whizzing bicycle and feeling the cool early-morning air on my bare arms and thinking again that my mother was wrong about it all, about getting up at dawn, about the exciting sense of purpose and a job – this was life.

22

What's Good for the Goose

ARRIVING THROUGH THE GATES of the old Palace Hotel I saw a scene of wonderfully frantic activity, with people dashing about and lots of huge trucks and trailers parked out front. Filming equipment was everywhere, with a big crane being set up and Tony Tenser and the director seated in real canvas director's chairs. It was where I most wanted to be in the world.

A girl with a clipboard told me to go and help myself to breakfast, pointing to a truck serving bacon and egg sandwiches. I sat at a table with a few other extras and actors. Everyone in 'What's Good for the Goose' was young: Sally, the star, was nineteen and several of the extras were teenagers. They were dressed for the 'disco scene', with one guy wearing flowered bell-bottom trousers and nothing but a tie over his bare chest.

Someone told me, 'Did you see them? The Pretty Things were just here, the real band; they've gone into hair and make-up.'

I turned to the boy in the tie. 'Wow, this film is so groovy!'

He gave me a withering look. 'Except that the lead is Norman Wisdom!'

I had to admit Norman wasn't the coolest, though I'd only seen him in one film, when he did something very silly with a ladder.

I got back that evening and excitedly told my mum and Peter all about my day.

'Norman Wisdom wrote it himself, and he's this boring banker at a conference in Southport, who gets mixed up with a hippy girl and goes for a sail on the sea of love.'

Peter frowned at this, but my mum thought it was funny.

'The hippy girl is Sally Geeson, she's gorgeous,' I raved.

My mother raised her eyebrow, 'Wishful thinking! She's hardly any older than you.'

Peter asked if there was any nudity in the film. I said that I'd been told there was some 'skinny dipping' but I wouldn't be in that scene.

In a fit of optimism, Jane and I went around the neighbours', posting letters through doors inviting people to our garden party, and we rather boldly put 'Opened by film star Norman Wisdom' at the top. I suggested to my mother that she pretend it was her idea, the charity part, and she rolled her eyes, but seemed to see that it might not be a bad move.

Towards the end of our filming, I saw what looked like a good moment to catch Norman.

'Don't ask, don't get' and the ant and his rubber tree went through my head.

I walked over to where he was sitting in the hotel reception.

'Mr Wisdom. I just wanted to say what a big fan of yours I am, and how much I loved being part of this film.'

He nodded graciously, and told his assistant to give me one of his signed pictures.

'There is one other thing. I'm holding a charity event for the League of Pity.' Peter had suggested this wording. 'And I wondered if you could spare a few minutes of your time on Saturday to be our star guest. My house is only down the road and it would mean so much to us all if you could make a brief appearance.'

He turned to his PA. 'How's Saturday looking?'

'It's mainly "pick-up shots",' she said, 'but we should get a break.'

We left it that we would wait and see, but the assistant gave me a big wink and a thumbs-up.

It was enough to update our publicity material. Jane and I wrote many more announcements saying the date was now this Saturday with a 'confirmed visit from film star Norman Wisdom, fresh from filming his new comedy.'

The grand opening was scheduled for 2 p.m. That morning Peter made a platform at the end of the garden for Jane's Rose Queen throne, which was a chair he covered in ivy. Then, miraculously, a few neighbours and local kids began arriving to help, in response to the leafleting I'd done along the street. A boy from up the road, Andrew Bentley, put up a tent and made a sign saying SIXPENCE FOR A KISS; he planned to sit in there all day selling kisses. One girl and her dad had made a treasure hunt in an old sandbox, another turned up with a fat baby and a sign saying GUESS THE WEIGHT OF THE

BABY and Ava wrapped tombola presents beautifully for her table. The garden was beginning to look convincingly like a fete but I heard my mother on the phone inviting Auntie Grace and saying that she was sure no one would come.

I set up my desk at the front gate with Jane's League of Pity money box, to charge an entrance fee. Just before two o'clock my mother came out looking worried. She had put lots of soft drinks behind the bar in the party room and set tables and chairs out everywhere. She looked down the empty road anxiously and then at her little gold watch. I wasn't concerned; it wasn't two o'clock yet.

At last, and just as her watch said two, the first people appeared in the distance, walking along the usually quiet road. Then a car drove up and parked, and then another. By two fifteen there was a steady stream of people and cars that built up to a crowd, and my mother had to sit next to me to help with taking money as a long queue formed and the street was lined with vehicles.

Peter came out and took over as ticket seller, and I said once again what a brilliant idea it was of Mummy's to do this for charity.

Then I went out to the back garden where a proper party was now in full swing. The fat baby was being passed along, people were waiting to place flags in the sandpit. There was a rush for Ava's tombola and she looked so wonderful in her white lace dress and huge white hat that I felt they were queueing up to look at her more closely.

The only less than successful contribution was Andrew who emerged from the hot tent looking very red in the face and bemused as to why no one was willing to wait for a kiss.

What made me very happy was that my mother looked like a normal mummy and all the neighbours were being so friendly to her. It was as if it was her party, and people were congratulating her on her lovely home and garden and saying that she must come around for a cup of tea. Perhaps her years of social exclusion were finally over.

In the middle of it all, Peter appeared with Norman Wisdom and everyone cheered. He stood at the doors of the party room and Peter called, 'All quiet please!'

The hubbub stopped and Norman shouted, 'I declare this garden party open and wish it a great success. And hope you will all come to see our film. Thank you, Southport, for your warm welcome!'

He was about to leave but my mother rushed up to him and began chatting; suddenly he changed his mind and disappeared with her into a corner of the party room where I saw him mesmerized.

That evening Peter told me that he'd been 'very impressed' and I felt that we had bonded over the whole event. At dinner we began to chat about my interests, and I made an extraordinary discovery. It seemed that Peter and I had a lot in common, and as I talked about reincarnation I realized that he knew a lot about it. We became so animated that my mother began to laugh and said that we were made for each other as I was Miss Crazy Pants and he was Mr Bananas. Perhaps we were made for each other, as these conversations were the most exciting I had ever had with an adult, and yet this was a man I had at first struggled to talk to. I'd been searching for something and now, amazingly, it seemed that Peter might be the person to supply it.

The filming was almost finished, and I only managed to speak to Tony Tenser one more time. I thanked him for the wonderful experience and asked his advice about becoming a film producer or director. He said that the important thing was to work hard at school and pass all my exams first.

In retrospect this may have just been an adult saying what he thought he should say to a young person. After all, he'd made his own way up by working at ABC cinemas before getting himself into the publicity department and having a stream of brilliant ideas, one of the most inspired being to get a waxwork of Brigitte Bardot made, and then hiring someone to steal it, a stunt which got her name and picture into every newspaper in Britain. He became the nearest thing Britain had to a movie mogul, and with little education behind him. But I didn't know any of this at the time, and his words planted in my mind the seeds of a terrible idea. It hadn't occurred to me that my brilliant future might be hampered by not having been to school much. Despite having read as widely as many literature graduates, I could barely add up and had no hope of passing any exams.

Oddly this marked a turning point for me, and despite it coming during a moment of happy success, it filled me with a new anger and sense of rebellion. I'd always tried to help my mother, particularly with her boyfriends, and even now with making a good impression on Peter. She hadn't been helping me, though. My terrible education was all her fault; the fact that I could not do things like swim or hold a tennis racket was all down to her. I was weird, and I'd had a weird childhood. She was weird and had left me with strangers; she didn't even deserve Peter, or a normal life.

These revelations seemed to crash in on me, one after another. If I'd felt like an awkward, odd child it was because she had dominated me so much. She'd let me miss school because it kept me in her power, and I might have found my own way of educating myself, but that would never qualify me to do all these wonderful jobs that *The Young Eve* talked about. My desire to escape from her now became overwhelming and I was determined to find a way.

I was more desperate than ever that the wedding should take place.

It was now clear to me that I had spent years worrying about my mother, and taking care of her, and that the marriage would allow me to be free. But I was beginning to feel more and more sorry for Peter as I got to know him, and I very much wanted to believe that she would make him happy.

A few weeks before the wedding date Audrey announced that she would have to go into hospital. Something called fibroids had been detected in her womb and so she was to have an operation, a hysterectomy, and would be away from home for several days, but I wasn't to worry. Auntie Grace would move in to look after me, and Peter would bring me to the hospital to visit. So one evening he picked me up and we drove over to the Southport General Infirmary. After parking the car he turned off the engine. I sensed he wanted to say something, as he sat there shyly.

I started filling the silence with my chatter about a film I'd just seen. 'So there's this big black well sort of thing, and the apemen start behaving more like humans when they are near it. Then there are these astronauts, and one is a computer called Hal that speaks to them like this. "I'm sorry, Dave". . .'

He muttered something about it sounding interesting. He turned to face me, his colour coming back as he found his courage, then turned again to stare out of the windscreen.

'About your mother . . . you see, Sally,' he steadied himself, 'I knew that some lucky people had what you might call a "grand passion" and I thought I would be definitely the last man on earth that would ever happen to . . . until that day when you and your mother walked, or should I say crashed, into my kitchen.'

He looked at me with a sudden flood of feeling. 'It's been quite a shock, to tell you the truth.'

He waited for a reaction, and I managed to smile and say that this was lovely news.

Then we went into the hospital. I felt a rush of sympathy for him mingled with foreboding.

23

The Wedding

THE MORNING CAME AT LAST, and my mother appeared in her wedding outfit, a cream suit and a hat with lots of tiny fragile feathers on it, swaying in the breeze. She had lost weight and was now a little thin for the jacket, and her face looked delicate, framed by all the feathers. At the altar I stood behind her and watched her shaking in fear. The hat and feathers trembled in sympathy, revealing her panic to the whole congregation. I heard Auntie Grace mutter to Phil, 'I'm surprised he isn't the one quaking in his shoes.'

My mother and Peter then disappeared off on their honeymoon to Malaysia, where Peter had recently signed a lucrative deal to sell sweets. On their return they showed me photographs of them against white beaches and turquoise sea, and having drinks on wide painted verandahs, and with backdrops of enormous green frondy leaves. In these pictures Peter had a lovely big smile, a smile I hadn't seen before, which transformed him into a handsome man.

My mother seemed delighted that she could now go with him on something called business trips, where she would

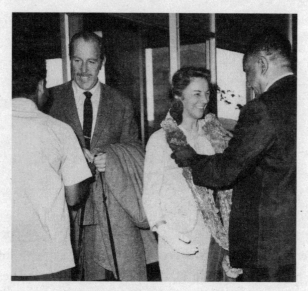

Mum and Peter on their honeymoon.

travel in a rather different style than before. Now she would at last be like the lady we had met on the cruise ship, the wife with the devoted husband fetching her wrap when she felt cool, taking care of her. I remembered her appearing in front of Auntie Grace in that glittering swimsuit with all the feathers coming out of her bottom, and I wondered, does she even know how to be this other person? And will she be able to love Peter?

Peter didn't appear to expect very much at first, but he did hope for some kind of home life. It wasn't clear whether he had known quite how completely unable my mother was to do anything of a domestic nature. I had a vague memory of her trying once to boil me an egg, but otherwise I'd never seen her cook anything.

One evening, soon after they'd returned, I came home to find her almost in tears. She was trying to mop the floor with tea towels, and it was an ice rink. She had put a large chicken in to roast with nothing underneath it, and the fat had seeped out of the bottom of the oven and spread in a film across the lino.

She said crossly, 'The butcher said I could just stick it straight in the oven as it was, and now look what's happened.'

I helped her transfer it into a suitable oven tray and clean up, but she was determined that it was because she 'wasn't the domestic type' and nothing could change. She frowned when I read to her from *The Young Eve*: 'Once upon a time people thought it charming for a girl to pretend she was helpless and couldn't hold a pan . . . now, from duchesses to dustmen, the idea is the same – cooking matters!'

'Oh, you and your *Girls' Guide*, it will turn you into a bore if you don't look out!' she said irritably.

It hardly mattered, as I was beginning to see that Peter was still so devoted to her he would have lived on chip butties for ever and there was no reason to worry. Perhaps she had got away with it, and he would just accept everything about her. It would be unfair, though, to depict him as simply under her spell. Peter managed to be totally moral and also the least judgemental man imaginable. He was that rare thing: a completely kind person.

Peter now said enthusiastically that he would do the cooking, as he had always cooked for himself anyway. His repertoire was simple; he would grill a lamb chop or fillet steak and serve it with frozen chips and peas or sweetcorn.

There were also, for the first time now in the late Sixties, ready meals and deep-freeze delights that he would try out. Findus Crispy Pancakes oozed interesting fillings to mop up with your chips. Vesta Chow Mein was a miracle in a packet which included what appeared to be flat strips of white plastic that, when dropped in hot oil, puffed up into crunchy yellow noodles. Smash created mashed potato by just adding water to a powder. There was something fascinating about these futuristic instant dishes that my mother loved: more like food that you would eat in a space capsule and nothing to do with drudgery and dull housewives. In the TV advert for Smash there were goofy-looking aliens tittering at the silly Earthlings who were actually *peeling* potatoes, and my mother had more in common with these little green men than with the women who she disdainfully called 'the domestic type'.

Keith was back at boarding school, but he came home in the holidays and we had a strange attempt at family life. I was surprised to see how much Peter now smiled. He had a nice, kind face, and could look what my mother called 'distinguished'. He was tall, and Audrey said he looked like Steed in *The Avengers* and bought him a bowler hat, which he obediently wore to go to work. I realized that he would have worn a pink bonnet if she had asked him to.

Life with Peter was like watching someone shed something, an outer chrysalis of stiff, stoical unhappiness. Inside was this entirely different man who could do a perfect impersonation of Sean Connery as James Bond, who could laugh till tears appeared in his eyes, and join in with the chorus of

Peter, 1969.

'Lovely Weather for Ducks' while my mother did one of her dance routines across the kitchen floor.

Keith later told me that the most surprising moment of his whole life was coming back from school and going into the living room that first summer to find his father with my mother sitting on his knee. She was gently flicking his ear, kissing it and singing, '*Little Peter Rabbit had a fly upon his ear, so he flipped it and he flopped it and the fly flew away*,' while Peter giggled. In short, we both realized that they were happy and transformed by that happiness.

Suddenly everything had changed. My mother would wait for the sound of his key in the door. He had, rather shyly, suggested that I might call him Daddy, and he would walk in and shout, 'It's the Daddy man!' She would run over to wrap her arms around him, and they would reach out to me and I'd join them – only to find in myself an unexpected reluctance. It seemed that, almost overnight, I'd changed too.

There was a terrible irony, of course, in that for so many years I had longed for normal childhood and now, just as it finally arrived – the family I had so wished for, the house I'd always imagined – I found that all I wanted was to get away.

One of my greatest problems at that age was what to do during school hours. Despite Tony Tenser's terrible warning I still couldn't bear to sit in classes where I was so behind. My mother would announce the day with a song, and I'd roll out of bed to strains of 'Be My Little Baby Bumblebee', with Audrey buzzing around, and even pulling back the covers to buzz in my ear.

'Oh shhh . . .' I'd say grumpily.

Peter had pointed out that Mr Moore's taxi was hardly necessary when there was a bus stop near the house, so I would now pull on the hideous maroon school blazer, and set off in the right direction, rolling up the waistband of my skirt as I walked. In my pencil case was the make-up I would thickly apply as soon as I'd made my dash for freedom. Then I would either shirk school altogether or I'd arrive and go into assembly, sing hymns, then shuffle into the classroom, daydream till break, and then find my legs carrying me out of the school and down the road into town. If the school called my mother she would say I had tummy ache and had come home.

'It's my fault,' she would declare, 'life's been too exciting for you. Just don't tell Daddy,' and she would sing:

'How ya gonna keep her locked up in school,
after she's seen Paree?'

She was more than disinterested in education; she actually resented it. She still believed that it might impede a girl's chance of catching a man, or the right sort of man.

Despite the tacit permission, the process of truancy always felt creepily trancelike, especially as I now feared it might have ruined my life, and having got away from the school I was always plagued by the same uncertainty about what I could possibly do with my days.

In summer there was the distraction of the sea-front and Pleasureland. I'd always loved the gaudy grubby madness of the fairground, but now I'd noticed a new attraction – the bikers who worked there. They were a dreamily rough bunch and I loved to watch how, if there were pretty girls aboard, they would send the Waltzer into a frenzied spin, the cars whirling with shrieks of fear, all whizzed up with the train-track rattle and blaring overloaded speakers with their cacophony of the latest pop hits.

I'd once had a moment of wild success when I'd got talking to one of the bikers, Jeff. He was big and surly, so it was fun to try to get him to smile and show a glint of his gold tooth. I loved to imagine us setting off together on a road trip across America on his motorbike, the wind in my hair as we rode through Monument Valley.

There was an indoor Fun House at the fair that was a great pick-up place for teenagers, like a giant playground for adults, with dark cubicles where you could go in to see Lady Godiva or Peeping Tom. Jeff at last caught my look, and followed me into one of the cubicles and pushed a fat tongue into my mouth and moved it around. He then fondled my padded bra, before working out that I didn't have breasts and pulling away nervously. He peered at me in the darkness, realizing that under my thick make-up I was no more than a kid. But it didn't matter that he'd recoiled; I was still triumphant.

On a weekday, however, or in wet weather, all my usual hang-outs were closed and depressing. The sea was receding year by year and the beach was now a mudflat stretching wetly to a distant grey ocean. Southport, the wonderland of my childhood, was slowly disappearing and in its place was a dull seaside town that even the sea had abandoned.

So what to do? Occasionally there would be an 'adventure', an old man in a shelter I could 'tease' in my hitched-up skirt and thick eyeliner, a wannabe Lolita. Most of these men could be taken to the point where they would do or say something inappropriate; in one case the man unzipped his flies. But it stopped there, with a thrill on both sides, and then I ran away.

Then the holidays arrived, and it was the long, hot summer of 1971, which seemed to be teeming with gorgeous, erotic images of love in the long grass. We cooled off in the darkness of the cinema watching *The Go-Between* with Julie Christie and came out panting over Alan Bates. We drooled over Cat Stevens on *Top of the Pops*, and covered our rooms with pictures of him. We read D. H. Lawrence avidly, and dreamt of Cat Stevens doing to us whatever the gamekeeper Mellors had done to Lady Chatterley.

We, for I had found a best friend at last, with whom I now spent every day. Cath's mother had died and her father, a vicar, and a man with a vague bewildered air that may have been grief, gave her as much freedom as my own distracted mother gave me. When anyone asked what I was doing I would mention cinema trips, books, or staying at Cath's house. I had a door key and the magic purse, and no one ever bothered to determine the boundaries.

Cath and I now spent most of our time looking for trouble. It was in some ways a further frustration that the adults weren't interested in us. We could be outrageous, take trains to distant places, stay out late, and all we were faced with was the inescapable and depressing fact that still nothing exciting happened. I was stuck, with no sense of how to escape and a growing panic that my future might have been ruined by my mother and my lack of schooling. My best chance of getting away from her was clearly to have a boyfriend who would carry me off.

Our favourite activity, often fruitless, was looking for hippies. They had suddenly invaded Southport the summer of 1969, and since then had hung out and played guitars on the steps of the Monument in town. This previously dull landmark had instantly taken on an aura of counter-culture mystique, enhanced by the fact that the local schools had placed a ban on pupils being in its vicinity while in uniform.

So, one day of that endless hot summer, we went through my jumble-sale hoard and dug out long silky dreses, flowing scarves and beads in which we might pass as hippy girls and we wandered into town. Sadly the steps were deserted, so we trudged past possible coffee bars, looking into them hopefully in our unconvincing costumes. It was now early evening but the muggy heat had brought on desperation. Cath had to go home so I trudged on alone. At last I walked past the Wimpy bar and there was someone who was not only a hippy but almost as gorgeous as Cat Stevens or Chris.

Chris had been my first hippy. He lived in a dirty squat near the promenade and was painfully thin. I took him fillet steaks, stolen from the household deep freeze, which thawed out, leaking sweet-smelling watery blood into the bottom of my school satchel. I then cooked them ineptly on his filthy cooker, and in return he made me a patchwork velvet bag that was my favourite possession for years. But as I barely had breasts and as he was probably quite old and probably a junkie, things never took off romantically.

I now went into the Wimpy and sat down. The man looked even more thrilling in close-up. He was older than Chris but had thick black hair hanging down his back, a beard, and pink loon pants. Wrapped around his neck was a bedraggled feather boa. I rummaged in the patchwork bag and pulled out a slightly crumpled cigarette, walked over and asked him for a light.

'Love the boa,' I said. 'Where's it from?'

He waggled it. 'Yeah, from Kensington Market.'

'How fabulous. I miss London terribly. I just live to go to London,' I said dramatically.

'Come, if you like. I'm going back there in the morning,' he said. 'I'll give you a lift, but it'll have to be early, I've got a job on.'

We chatted a bit and then I told him I'd meet him outside the café the next day. I went to a phone box and called Cath to tell her the plan. 'So if anyone asks where I am tomorrow night, say I'm staying at yours, OK?'

She balked a little at this. 'What if they want to speak to you?'

'You know they never check, and if they do just say that I'm on my way over. Then, if I don't turn up, you can pretend you thought I'd changed my mind.'

She was fine with that, so I went home to pack a small bag and plan my trip. The next morning I sneaked out leaving a note 'gone for early morning bike ride, staying at Cath's' and went back to wait. At last his car pulled up and I jumped in, then he roared off, the radio on and a stash of ready-rolled joints on the dashboard. I was in heaven.

24

Breaking Away

LONDON HAD NEVER SEEMED more like the Promised Land, as I stepped from the sunshine of the King's Road into Stop the Shop's inky-black interior, with its floor revolving to the sound of the Supremes and mannequins appearing to slow-dance to 'Love Child'. The guy with the boa didn't spike my drink or have sex with me. He just listened happily to my prattle as we drove down the motorway and then left me where I asked to be left, on the King's Road, and gave me a key to a flat in Earls Court and his girlfriend Eliza's phone number. He said I could stay on their sofa.

That night, happy and exhausted, with my magic purse almost empty, I finally trudged back to the address scrawled on the scrap of paper with a smudgy map. It had been a perfect day of King's Road, Carnaby Street and shopping. I rang the doorbell, clutching my bags of booty, suddenly nervous of what I might find. Eliza was there, enviable Eliza with her tangled locks and her hippy boyfriend. She fed me vegetable bake and asked me the truth about how old I was, and then very firmly told me to ring my mother straight away.

They were already in bed, and my mother was in the hall in her nightie keeping her voice down, hoping Peter wouldn't catch on. She thought I was sleeping at Cath's; where on earth was I? She sounded seriously rattled as I explained. Eliza spoke to her, and apologized, saying it had been a misunderstanding. Eliza seemed worried enough about her boyfriend's complete idiocy in taking an underage girl with him that she was willing to lie for me, but she landed me in it by saying that I had told her I was older. When she offered to put me on a train home the next morning my mother calmed down.

But back home I overheard Audrey and Peter talking about what to say to me. It was the first time that I'd heard him angry with her.

'She's barely thirteen. She could have been abducted – anything could have happened. How can she believe that this was acceptable behaviour?'

Her voice was low and I couldn't make out her words, just a sad mumble.

'You are the mother,' he said. 'You have to show her who is boss.'

It seemed to be dawning on him that she lacked the confidence to really discipline me. Having made me her partner in crime for so many years, she felt she had no authority to begin parenting me properly now.

Peter now began an attempt at a clampdown. I would have to always let them know where I was – a simple rule, but one that left me feeling full of rage and frustration. I'd been leading my own life for years and no one had cared.

Now, when it suited him, he had decided to treat me like a child. He began to notice things he had previously over-looked, commenting on my clothes and 'the stuff on my eyes' and what was and wasn't 'suitable'. The result was to make me more determined than ever to get away from this suffocating attempt at family life. London became my new goal, and although I was only thirteen I was determined to get there as soon as possible. In the meantime I wanted a boyfriend and to have sex.

The Wimpy bar where I had met my hippy was down by the seafront and had big sticky plastic tomatoes on the tables and condensation running down the windows. Inside this cosy fug Cath and I would now daily meet the boys from the King George V Grammar School, known as KGV. Even if I hadn't been to school that day, I would still turn up to meet the other girls fresh out of the classroom, and we would trail together down to the Wimpy. These boys weren't as interesting as hippies – many had spots and lacked any social grace – but they were available.

One day my mother appeared at the café window, peering through the steamy glass and waving. She walked in, entirely incongruous in her mink-lined raincoat with diamanté buttons, smiling warmly at everyone as if they were the most charming gathering she had ever seen. She put her arm around me and asked how I was. She had been worried about me as I had started my periods that morning. I was fine, and she now announced gaily to the group of pimply youths, 'My little girl is a woman!' and then swept out.

We celebrated my womanhood by piling into the 'pin-nies', the amusement arcade next door with its pinball machines that the boys would play frenziedly in those days before computer games. We, the girls, would compete for who could look on with the greatest admiration at their bril-liance. American girls may have had to wave pom-poms and kick their legs; in Southport you just had to stand at the pinnies and not look too bored.

As well as Cath, I had another new friend, Amy, who was part of this Wimpy-bar gang, and I realized she was fantastic boy bait. Now that I was a teenager I was confident I would one day develop wonderful pert breasts like hers, but they were yet to arrive. Amy also had big blue eyes, a blonde mane and a sweet nature. The boys would come to kneel at her shrine and I could pick them off with my more-compelling personality and vamping techniques.

My mother had little sense of childhood, and simply saw it as an inconvenient life stage to be got through as quickly as possible. Her announcement to the local grammar-school boys that I was technically now a woman had been a sign of genuine relief. I was launched and now a fellow traveller rather than a small needy person and she was delighted to share any womanly wisdom with me. She seemed to me at this time to be an unfathomable combination of needing to control me, and wanting me to be her. I didn't believe she knew herself what she really wanted.

One thing that I was keen to learn was how to catch a man. I'd already absorbed a lot, partly from observation and from tips that I had heard her pass on to other women, secret spells for spinning a gossamer web of attraction that was supposed to settle over a man and hold him entranced. Now that I was older she was sharing the precious secrets of this female sorcery with me and, as she liked to point out, 'Your *Eve's Guide for Girls* book won't tell you about this!'

She seemed to be right, as the chapter in *The Young Eve* called 'Being Beautiful' assured that any girl who is 'reasonably proportioned and healthy, who is glad to be alive and tiptoe with eagerness to know about everything' would have men falling at her feet. My own observations of Southport youth suggested that this wasn't always the case, so I now took careful note of the Audrey method.

She demonstrated the delicate operation of 'making them fall in love' as a kind of dance: one moment you were up close to them, smiling right into their eyes thinking wonderful thoughts; the next you were wafting away from them, so that they were waiting for you to come back. She explained how to ask them about the things they most loved talking about, and to then cup your hand under your chin and listen to them with a fascinated expression.

'People most enjoy talking about their best life moments,' she would say, after listening with great enthusiasm to some man describing how, as a child, he would revamp old motorbikes together with his dad. 'It makes them feel happy and they then associate that happy glow with you.

'If you want them to actually fall in love with you, then just as you have been in rapt attention, you should suddenly look away, very mysteriously, into the distance and sigh with soulful eyes. They will ask you what you are thinking, and you just softly say, "I was wondering . . . oh nothing really." They are left wondering. That is the pulling-away part of the dance.

'Then you just sigh and pick up where they left off. "So, what were you saying about your rugby match – how exciting!" You need to get their head spinning, slightly disoriented, and then comfortable again. They need to feel you are partly their best chum and partly this magical and mysterious creature that they will never fully know or understand.'

Then there were other ingredients one should sprinkle into the love potion: creating a picture that they can hold in their minds, that they can remember as the moment they 'fell in love'. This could be on a dance floor – 'though not in your case', she was quick to add. It could just be a walk down a staircase, or a moment that you turn and toss your hair, and meet their eyes, but it needs to be thought about and worked on.

Another essential component in Audrey's arsenal was making a man feel like the centre of the world as you constantly say his name. 'People love to hear their own name, but say it as if it is a lovely sound – Julian or Roger or Brian – as if it was music.' This made me giggle, but Cath and I nonetheless practised saying the names of the boys we knew as if they were music: 'Eric Crankshaw . . . Terry Woolley . . .' we would intone in breathy voices.

They need to feel that they are your hero, my mother told me. You should repeat things that they've told you as if they were terribly wise. Also make them feel important and useful by giving them something to fix, like a problem or a flat tyre;

and of course, make them laugh or, even better, find *their* jokes terribly funny. My mother and I specialized in terrible jokes, so we now practised telling each other the worst jokes we could think of, and then trying to make our laughs like the peal of tiny bells.

Dave was the prettiest boy I had seen, with blond hair to his shoulders and a handsome chiselled face, and the first time that we met him, he had made a beeline for Amy. They had now been going out for a week, but the following Friday night there was a party, followed by a cricket-club dance on Saturday and the youth club on Sunday: a whole weekend of close proximity. Amy would of course take me along, so this would give me ample time for theft, and I rehearsed all of the tricks with great thoroughness. At the party Amy stood by him as I asked questions about the cricket scores, and then, having milked that topic, I listened fascinated to his description of his mother's new car. I looked in awe and admiration at the way he could twirl a coin between his fingers. I laughed and laughed at the names he invented for the host's home-brew beer. I said the name 'Dave' with a special tone of excited warmth, and when Amy went to the loo I began smiling into his eyes, telling him all about my job as an extra on the film, and how thrilling it had been.

'It's like you were saying the other day, Dave, about how money is freedom. I thought about that afterwards, it's so true.'

Then, as I had reeled him in, the pulling away. I suddenly looked off into the distance and sighed soulfully.

'What's the matter, Sally, are you OK?' said Dave.

'Oh, it's just something . . . oh, nothing . . . I was just thinking . . .'

Then Amy came back from the loo. Dave was looking at me oddly.

'I'll just go into the garden for some air,' I said. 'I find looking at the stars so calming.'

I wasn't surprised when Dave appeared in the garden a few minutes later.

'Are you all right?'

'Yes, Dave, I've been having a difficult time at home, but being around you makes me feel so much safer, as if everything is somehow going to be OK.' I stared into his eyes as if he was my saviour and could fix my broken life, there being no broken bicycle handy.

By the end of the weekend I had stolen him from her and the big tears rolled down Amy's lovely cheeks as she agreed that nothing could be done if he 'loved me more'.

It was only then I realized that Audrey's ruthlessness was there in me too. Her power was beginning to bloom in me, along with my woman's body, and I wasn't sure that it was a rose or a daisy so much as some monstrous flytrap. I had the terrifying thought that I might one day become her, but the heady excitement of my power over men was too strong to resist. I was no longer the small boring person in our double act; I had deployed her tricks, and been every bit as effective as she might have been, which left me feeling triumphant.

Since the incident with Peter's gatepost I was more aware than ever of how brilliantly effective her ingenuity and fierce determination could be.

I watched her swing into operation with poor Keith, who had arrived back from his boarding school the week before, looking overweight and unhappy. He wouldn't go out and have fun, as directed. Instead he thwarted her, by sitting in front of the television, fat, hot and cross. After a few days of this my mother signed him on at the tennis club as, despite her dislike of sports, she could think of no other solution to his lack of a social life. She bought him tennis clothes and a racket, despite his muttering, 'No way am I playing tennis.'

The next day there we were. I was sitting in the back of the car, Keith in the front next to my mother, as she roared up the road to the dreaded tennis club. He was staring out of the window glumly; no one spoke.

We arrived outside the club, and she waited. He went on sitting there, in dangerous defiance.

'Go on, get out.'

He still sat there, and I knew what was coming.

'Get out of this bloody car and play tennis,' she said in a voice that froze the blood.

I saw him flinch. He at last climbed out.

'I'll collect you at five o'clock.'

He stomped off in misery.

When he got home for dinner, sweaty and miserable, a plate was put in front of him with nothing but a Ryvita and a dollop of cottage cheese and lettuce leaf. We were all on a diet, apparently, in support of him, and there was no other food in the house. Peter had resorted to having a sandwich at the golf club before he came home.

Keith took one look at his plate and furiously stormed out of the kitchen before slamming the door.

She would not relent and became more determined than ever. Each day there was a new scene. By the end of that summer Keith was transformed; he was now slim, tanned, attractive and playing tennis happily every day before going out to have fun with his new girlfriend. The rows were forgotten. Peter and I both looked on in awe and admiration.

The juggernaut of Audrey's will mowed down everything in its path, and as long as it was getting you to where you wanted to be, that was fine. There was no better person to have on your side. But these days I could see it more clearly, the sheer size of it, and I was shocked to find rising up in me a strong desire to resist this force, to become just as powerful, and to show her what wonders I could achieve on my own.

THE TIMING OF THE boyfriend theft from Amy had been particularly mean and particularly clever, as Dave and his parents were going on a holiday, and now they invited me to join them. It would be a proper holiday, which didn't involve the shrimping nets and apple orchards so longed for in my childhood, but instead was all about my new jet-set aspirations of discos and sun loungers by the pool. Surprisingly, Peter didn't seem worried by any of this, and he now backed off in the belief that Dave and I were in the throes of an innocent teenage romance.

In fact, a few weeks before the holiday I had borrowed the keys to a friend of Cath's caravan near the beach in

Formby and taken Dave there. There had been heavy pet-
ting on the sofa, but now I wanted to move on to the real
thing. The caravan site was a long walk from the station,
through the gloomy pinewoods that had once been the scene
of my mother's heartbreak. When we opened up the caravan it was still dank after its winter abandonment. We made
tea, and lay on the damp bed. Dave seemed nervous and I
found the whole thing uncomfortable, and somewhat dis-
appointingly my magic button was totally overlooked in the
whole business. However, the attempt at adulthood seemed
to have bonded us, and we walked back through the woods
conscious that some rite had been undertaken.

My mother looked on happily, eager to see me getting
started and putting into action the many life lessons she
believed she had instilled in me. She had never been very
interested in my childhood clothes, but now we would drive
into Liverpool where we crammed into changing rooms as
she enthusiastically dressed me up in outfits that made me
look older, and we splashed out on make-up and underwear.
She bought me a set of knickers with slogans like 'Please,
please me' on them and thought it was hilarious.

On Saturday nights Dave and I would now come home
from meeting friends in the pub to watch *Match of the Day*
on the television in our downstairs party room, and we
would shag, in an unimaginative teenage way, to the rousing
rhythms of the closing theme tune. At one point my mother
would shout down the stairs, 'Get your knickers on,' and
bring us a tray bearing that Seventies treat of two cups of
Nescafé made with frothy milk. I don't remember whether

the sex was pleasurable or not; it was a badge of honour and I imagined that the more we did it the better we would get at it. Dave was sweetly dedicated to being a good boyfriend, polishing up his mother's white Vauxhall Viva before picking me up on a Friday night, taking on a Saturday job so that he could buy me the weekly Mixed Grill and an Irish coffee at the Fox and Goose Berni Inn, and saving up his No. 6 cigarette coupons for a locket he'd seen in the catalogue

As the holiday approached my excitement rose, and soon Dave, his mum and dad and I were all on the plane heading to the Spanish resort of Benidorm, me reeking of my new Kiku perfume. Dave had bought this at duty free, and on the flight he whispered breathily in my ear 'Faberge made love and called it Kiku.' Everything about that holiday seemed the height of adult sophistication and way more exotic than any of the places I had travelled to with my mother. Fiji and Borneo paled beside the flowering oleanders and dark back-street bars of that Spanish town with its resort hotels and heady aroma of Ambre Solaire and cheap scent. At night we went to Tito's disco with our holiday friends – Ken was a London cabbie and Estelle a beautician who gave me a makeover, false eyelashes and all – and we'd sway back drunkenly through the warm air to the hotel. It was heaven: no Mummy, just me all grown up with my very own man.

We got home to what felt like a perfect teenage summer. There were Friday-night dances at a tennis or cricket club, or the church hall. The girls would dance around their handbags in a circle; the boys would play air guitar with their eyes closed. We bopped about to Mungo Jerry's 'In the

Summertime'; if they lowered the lights and played T. Rex it felt decadent, and at the end of the evening we would find our mate and slow-dance to something like Herman and the Hermits' 'My Sentimental Friend'. On Sunday nights we piled into Vince's three-wheeler, which stank of Brut aftershave, and listened to the radio play the top hits with a countdown to number one. Then we arrived at the youth club to smuggle in Vince's father's home-made brew, known as Old Fart, and play ping-pong and taunt the skinheads.

The days went by in a happy haze of lying on rugs in the sand dunes, with languid afternoons listening to more sophisticated rock music in our party room – Cream and Led Zeppelin – and then wandering into town to pubs and coffee bars just for the sake of going somewhere.

My mother was constantly in the wings of this new teen-age life, wanting to join in or give me advice. She made it clear that, while Dave was a nice boy, we were aiming for something much greater than this, although I had no idea what she imagined. She just needed to feel involved, and I would catch her peering in through the windows of the cricket club as we danced, and I'd run out to see her driving off. I was often torn between wanting to include her and wanting to keep her out. At times there was perhaps a faint taste of revenge for all the occasions when she had made me feel excluded.

My dread of summer boredom had passed during those weeks, and I only felt a lazy contentment made possible by my sense that I was now a proper grown-up. I was sure that some foggily imagined amazing new life was about to begin.

But that Summer of Love was the summer of shagging and clumsily used condoms. I had ignored my missed period and for some weeks my breasts had been swelling. I woke in the night with waves of agonizing pain, sheets wet with blood. I reluctantly called my mother who summoned our kindly local GP, Dr Farnsworth. He knew us well and looked very grave as he sent us to the hospital to have the remains of my pregnancy dealt with.

The news that I'd been pregnant at the age of fourteen somehow galvanized Peter into action. He was appalled, and no longer able to watch from the sidelines. He had possibly worked out other things about my lack of schooling, and about our life before their marriage. Whatever the catalyst, there was a sudden change in the balance of power, and the chief effect of the unbalancing was the disastrous impact on my relationship with my mother.

25

Rebellion

IF MY MOTHER had been aware that I was taking off those 'Please please me' panties she had bought me she certainly didn't confess that fact to Peter. She played dumb and acted as shocked as he was. He was so horrified that she couldn't argue with the rules he now insisted on.

I was banned from seeing Dave, who was going off to Manchester University and a new life, despite his protestations that he would be faithful to me and 'wait'. I never for a moment considered waiting, and had already found someone else.

Phil was a printer at the *Southport Visitor*, and to my eyes quite perfect; he was a bearded, long-haired hippy and several years older than Dave. As an escort he was ideal, as he looked so grown up. We went off to London, and my *Honey* magazine diary from that year records: 'Went to a club near Piccadilly Circus, had breakfast in Soho.' But Peter was furious, and my mother was told to take immediate action. She discovered that Phil was desperate to go away on a trip to France with some mates, so she gave him a hundred pounds and my stepbrother Keith's camping equipment in return for going off and never seeing me again. I was shocked that he accepted.

My reaction to this was to behave as badly as possible. I had travelled through some gateway to the world beyond home, and I couldn't find my way back even if I'd wanted to. The house I'd been so delighted with, the family life I'd craved – normal meals around a kitchen table with a nice daddy looking after us – had all been realized . . . but too late.

Peter looked on in misery as I told him to fuck off, screaming, 'You aren't my father, stop telling me what to do!'

My feelings towards my mother were more confusing. I hadn't missed what I hadn't had; I hadn't blamed Audrey for being an unconventional mother or for making her way in the world as she did. I had mostly adored her, admired her and found her hugely entertaining and amusing. I had also, at times, found her jaw-droppingly selfish, wilful and demanding. Above all, I knew that I didn't want to be like her and that this was a danger. The force field of her will had been such a part of the air I breathed that I needed to escape it, but I had no idea where to go. There was fury that my own independent dreams of a bigger life might depend on an education that I'd now scuppered, so all that remained for me was to find a man who could take me away.

My school attendance had always been poor, but I now never went at all and instead spent my days hanging around the town looking for trouble. I smoked dope constantly and met a much older man, a drug dealer with a fancy car, and spent afternoons in his bed. I ran away to Manchester and was brought back by the police. I came home hours later to an ashen-faced Peter, and at one point I hit my mother, knocking her over. Rage would rise up in me at the sight of her.

My mother went through her own crisis, pale and unrecognizable, as if her power had somehow ebbed away. Peter just looked on, shocked at what was being revealed, but not knowing how to help us. My mother would suddenly get up from the kitchen table in tears at my coldness, or shut herself away in her bedroom. She felt some rewriting of our history was happening, behind her back, and didn't know how to defend herself. I remember once, not long after she and Peter had got married, hearing Grace call her 'a delinquent mother', and she wept at this and said that she was 'only trying to find us a future and someone to take care of us', and she had, hadn't she? She had found us a daddy.

During those months of unhappiness I felt that our hunt for love had never been about me. It had all been for her. Throughout those years, I reflected, I'd always been right there at her side, someone who loved her, and whom she could have loved back; but I was never enough. It wasn't me she wanted; it had never been me. She had wanted a man, someone who would take care of her and give her the life she was searching for. I wondered whether, as well as sharing my father's two left feet and bookish ways, I also shared his sad eyes: filled with the knowledge that she could never love us enough. Had I always been not good enough? Was I a mistake?

Me in my teens, Southport.

Then I managed to get pregnant again. I think it was an act of rebellion, a signal that I was an adult not a child, a desire to provoke change, and in some ways it worked. *The Young Eve*, with its delightful promises of a happy and successful life, now lay abandoned, languishing on the bookshelf with my once-loved novels and poetry books. I might have burnt them all if I'd thought of it, as they felt full of some false promise of a life I could never achieve.

The three of us drove in silence to Edgbaston on the outskirts of Birmingham, where the abortion clinic was buried in a residential area of huge impersonal houses. The doctor was rough with me as he examined me internally, and when I protested he said, 'If you are old enough to get into this

condition you are old enough to deal with the consequences.'
My mother hovered around me, paler and quieter than I'd
ever known her.

The night before the operation we stayed in a hotel
and I remember how Peter couldn't eat his meal, and had
to leave the dinner table and find a quiet corner of the
lounge where he sat with his head in his hands. My mother
looked guilty, clearly feeling she had brought this on him.
He had married her and taken on a lovely young daughter,
and within a couple of years that daughter had turned into
a monster.

It was at that moment that things changed for me. I saw
this man sitting almost in tears and realized that he really
cared. He wasn't upset for himself; he was upset for me. He
wasn't angry; he was terribly sad. This idea slowly took root
in my mind and then became inescapable. He was a nice,
kind man and he wanted to help me. The thought finally
penetrated the shell of teenage anger and self-absorption.

I remembered how far we had come to find him. The
travelling, the men, and how much I'd longed for a normal
father figure. My mother's search may have been driven by
her own needs, but hadn't I been on my own search too?
Now we had found what we had been looking for, just what
I had always desired, and here I was hurting him. He only
wanted to be 'the daddy man' and I wasn't letting him. I had
needed to be saved, and now I wasn't letting him save me.

When we got back home, he sat me down and offered me
a life. I remember the conversation clearly. He said that if I
carried on like this, I would never do the things I had once

talked about. He said I would be lucky to get any sort of job. His trump card was suggesting that I could go south, and not live with my mother any more. If I would let him coach me, and pass just four O levels, then I could go to a sixth-form college in Oxford where Keith, my stepbrother, was now at university. He would find me a room and pay an allowance into a bank account for me. And if I got a place at university he promised that I would find the life I was looking for. He said that I was clever enough to do any of the things I had talked about – to be a writer or film-maker, or put on plays – any life was possible, but this was the decisive moment.

The promise of independence swung it, and a growing desire to please him. My mother regarded us with pity, sometimes making unhelpful remarks about not turning me into a bluestocking. Her comment that 'men don't like women who are too clever' almost caused their first row. It was a rare thing for him to be so annoyed with her, but he couldn't conceal his displeasure. So she went quiet and simply looked on as this new plan unfolded. She was clearly horrified by the idea of my leaving home, but never believed it would happen. My recent anger had shocked her enough to allow Peter to take charge, but she told herself that this was just some horrible phase I was going through and she would soon win me back.

Peter drove me to Oxford to see the city in early summer. It was Eights Week, when students race rowing boats along the river and sit on grassy banks beneath weeping willows eating strawberries and drinking Pimm's. It was beautiful and seemed full of promise.

Looking back, I see how much this shy man had thought about how to handle me. He not only showed me the grander pleasures of the university colleges, but he also took me to a darkly romantic folk cellar and drove me through an area of squatted houses where the hippies roamed. We went to a student production of *A Midsummer Night's Dream* in a college garden with a huge magnolia tree from which Puck climbed down while Titania danced through the audience as we sat on blankets among candlelight.

By the time we got home to Southport I was more than convinced; I was dying to go there and would do anything to achieve it. Without this new passion for Oxford I would never have got through the following months. The long hours of tutoring at the dining table were agony at first. Peter tried in vain to explain some basic mathematics, and was horrified at my total ignorance of many subjects. Only my English essays seemed likely to get a good grade without much effort. He thought I might enjoy art history, so bought me lovely art books and took me on trips to Liverpool to explore the paintings in the Walker Art Gallery. As we talked about them, I became excited, finding that, with his gentle encouragement, I had things to say about them. He also found ways of making history more interesting to me, and gradually I began to love these sessions. They gave me the same feeling I'd had during those moments as a small child, when my father and I would be together in his darkroom, quietly sharing some activity or other.

My mother seemed sad and excluded, waiting restlessly

Me, happy at fifteen.

for me to come back into her orbit. She never believed that I would really go.

By the summer exams I was reasonably prepared and the O levels were attained. It was real; I was about to leave home and Southport for ever.

AT FIFTEEN I am taking the first steps along my own yellow brick road, and the towers of Oz are glittering ahead in the sunlight. Peter drives us all down in his big brown Mercedes, the boot and back seat piled with suitcases full of my jumble-sale costume collection. It takes several hours and my mother is pale and fretting, worried about the idea of ever doing this journey in her small Triumph Herald, but she doesn't like to drive a big car. Peter says that she has got the pair of us 'round the world and back' so should be able to drive herself to Oxford. Now he is settled into married life he is finding his voice, which is firm but gentle, with an edge of light teasing. I realize that she is feeling bereft, and my own anger ebbs away, now that I am leaving her behind. I suddenly adore her again, and feel that I will miss her terribly.

At last we arrive at a large red-brick house in North Oxford, with a driveway packed with cars and excited girls. They all seem unreal and slightly theatrical, with several astonishing beauties. My mother is looking around in wonder and I can see how she loves it all. She keeps remarking how everyone seems so much more glamorous than she expected. Her dislike of education and general suspicion of Oxford as a nest of bluestockings is quickly evaporating.

Peter is now struggling up the stairs of the big Victorian villa that houses the first-year sixth-form girls. He brings up the second load of my luggage to the room that I'll be sharing with three others, and I look at the narrow wardrobe wondering where to put it all. My mother can't bear to leave the theatre going on around her, a first act from which she will soon be cruelly taken away.

She has been busily finding out the names of all the more flamboyant-looking girls and making them laugh, and now whispers to me which ones I should be friends with. Finally, Peter manages to coax her away by suggesting tea by the river. She makes me promise to call her every night, and even has tears in her eyes. Are the tears just about leaving me?

Or are they because it isn't her who is about to live this amazing new life? I can't tell.

I begin to unpack quietly, pulling out of the cases my fur coats – some moth-eaten, some sumptuous – followed by the numerous ball gowns, silk kimonos and antique tea dresses. It isn't long before I'm surrounded by a group of girls looking on in wonder, as I explain about Southport jumble sales being such rich pickings. Soon there will be a constant queue to borrow things and I have the idea of giving each item a nickname to keep track of them. A fur coat with a big collar is called the Empress, another the Duchess, then the Lady, and the Tramp; my Forties trench coat is the Casablanca. I understand that they are a new kind of currency, one that brings instant popularity.

I now produce the star of the collection: the black off-the-shoulder dress my mother wore to have her dinner in New York as Queen for a Day. It has lots of tiny little buttons up the back and is cut to follow the hips down then curve into the knees and out again, in what my mother calls a fishtail. I can't resist spinning the tale that goes with it, and they all sit enthralled and won't let me stop. They hold the dress admiringly and I suddenly realize that Audrey, even as she drives north back up the motorway, has already woven her way into my new life.

I also see what a gift she is handing on to me with these, with our stories. This is my legacy . . . And now, at last, I can become the storyteller.

26

A Journey North

THE FIELDS SPEED BY US, the northern towns and country-side, and I watch the blur of it all, seeing it through my reflection in the train window: me alone, without her. We are headed for Southport, where, in a grassy suburban cemetery, someone will be digging my mother's grave. They will be out in this pale early-summer sunshine, shovelling up the earth to make a place for her.

It still seems unthinkable.

This train journey was taken so often, through all those years stretching from childhood to adulthood, with her sitting right here on the seat beside me. She would step onto the train and glance around the compartment, and see just the right person for us to sit across from. I wasn't allowed to help her with the case. It was a prop, part of her technique. She would struggle with it for a moment over someone's head, until they stood to offer assistance. Sometimes I would watch my reflection watching her as if it were a movie.

'So kind of you,' she would say, eyes sparkling, and by the time we pulled in to Lime Street station in Liverpool these various men, as invariably they were, would be telling me, in wonder, that they had never had such an entertaining journey.

That seems so recent, and yet here I am, my suitcase packed with the grey, not quite mourning, clothes of the modern funeral-goer, realizing too late that she would probably have preferred the drama of me in an elegant black evening dress and veil.

Audrey herself never lost her drama and chic. Back in Oxford, I had only been at the college for a few weeks when she reappeared in a vaporous halo of Youth Dew, to steal the limelight once again. She had presents for all my new girlfriends, individually wrapped with their names on. They each opened them to find inside a gold insect locket that hung on a chain and when you squeezed its back legs its wings would open to reveal a tiny watch.

'What do you get when you cross an insect with a rabbit?' asked Audrey. 'Bugs Bunny!' As the girls laughed, I felt a strange stab of jealousy at hearing our old worst-joke game being shared with them. 'Now you'll always know when it's time to have fun!' Athough the lockets were definitely odd, they wore them all the time, and loved them just as they loved Audrey.

I'd soon become a fixture on the landing of St Clare's, hogging the telephone to tell my mother the latest episode in my new adventure. Most girls had a call from a parent once a term, but every night someone would pick up the phone, and I would hear them laugh, and then call out with amusement, 'It's Audrey!' She knew most of the girls by name, with an instinct for those destined for fame or notoriety. 'How's Paula,' she'd ask, 'is she there? Put her on!' and I'd grumpily listen to Paula regaling my mother with some hilarious anecdote. Later Paula would achieve overnight celebrity by crashing into rock stars' dressing rooms and photographing them in their underpants, and then she wore a magnificent scarlet ball gown to marry Bob Geldof, with David Bowie at her side. I remember my mother holding up a *Daily Mail* magazine to show me Paula's dress, modelled on Scarlett O'Hara's.

'Look at that. I always knew *Paula* would make something of herself.' I understood that nothing I could achieve in my own career would ever match up to that red ball gown.

But, away from her, my confidence grew. It took time for me to learn that I was still in some ways an outsider, just as she had once felt herself to be. In those first weeks away from home I heard two girls talking outside my room, and one asked, 'What's her name, you know the girl who sounds like Cilla Black?' And the other giggled, 'Oh, Sarah' – I'd changed back to my christened name of Sarah instead of Sally, hoping it sounded posher – and in a hideous Liverpudlian whine she went on, 'I'm Sarah from Southport, and one day I'd like to own a boootique or be an air 'ostess,' at which they both shrieked in delight. Within weeks I was speaking like everyone else at the school.

A few years ago I was reminded of this when I overheard another conversation, this time in a dress shop near Harrods in London. I'd arranged to meet my mother in a boutique that she told me she often visited because of her friendship with the two ladies who worked there. When I arrived, these women were both at the desk, smartly dressed and well spoken, and as I glimpsed her through the shop window, happily walking towards us. They noticed her at the same moment, and one said, 'Oh God no, it's that funny little woman from Southport again,' and they both groaned.

This slight to her cut me deeply and brought back the faint whispered remarks I had heard throughout my childhood. They had felt so unjust, but I knew that they were all facets of her. She was so many things: a social climber and an imposter; a delinquent but loving mother; a good-time girl but a devoted wife; a fantasist, a dreamer and a romantic, and at the same time ruthlessly practical. I would never be able to quite pin her down, and perhaps I didn't need to.

But the fear of becoming her had been strong enough to galvanize me. It had been my rocket fuel during those early years. At first, I'd wandered Oxford in a dream, delirious with my new-found freedom, before I realized how powerfully I wanted those things she'd never had: the social acceptance, the career and some status that didn't depend on any man. This drove me to overcome my feral habits and finally work for my A levels, which I succeeded in getting, along with a place to study English literature at London University. By the time I started living in London my accent had in it barely any trace of Liverpool.

Now, across the train aisle are my own teenagers, and they make my youth seem so long ago. They are almost adults, but today they are behaving like excited children in their delight at being together on an outing. They notice me from time to time and then try to look solemn. They loved their nana and found her entertaining and funny, but for them this is all in the natural order of things. It is different for daughters, and for us only children.

It took a long time for me to really step out of my mother's shadow. In those early years in London, any thoughts of breaking away from her felt doomed from the outset, as the corrupting magic purse of my childhood was upgraded into something even more seductive – the cocoon of Carmel Court, a tall, thin cottage in a small cobbled courtyard off Kensington Church Street. The house had a tiny rooftop terrace from which you could glimpse the gardens on the roof of Biba, the fabulous Art Deco department store that had become my teenage mecca. Audrey loved Biba as much as I did, and she insisted that Peter bought a place for me to live that would also be somewhere they could 'occasionally' stay. Audrey and I would spend evenings in Biba's top-floor Rainbow Room where the Pasadena Roof Orchestra played Fred Astaire songs we could sing along to, or have tea in the roof garden where flamingoes wandered past fountains.

My feelings about her more than 'occasional' visits were mixed, as she still brought such a cloud of glitter dust in her wake; the lights would twinkle but the air could be hard to breathe. The shadowy neighbours in the dingy boarding house across the courtyard would now be variously revealed as Michael Mannion, the self-styled Bard of Kensington, or Miss Primrose Lane, an elderly former debutante fallen on hard times who made her own hats. I would come home to have her 'finds' of the day introduced to me – 'This is Spencer Harper the Third, Kentucky aristocracy, I thought he could stay?' – and there would be people laughing around the kitchen table, their stories wheedled out and made extraordinary.

When Peter and Audrey weren't staying, my friends would come to dinner and be surprised by the continual interruption of the phone ringing, not just once or twice, but several times in an evening. I would become agitated and have to admit that Audrey would be upset if I didn't answer. 'She calls every night,' I would tell them, 'but I'll call her back when you leave.' It was only later, amid the exhaustion of my own family life and career, that it became a necessity to wean her off that daily contact.

Once I'd finally moved away from her orbit, I became increasingly aware of the desperate patterns I seemed doomed to repeat. We learn the steps so well, the choreography of this complex dance of our parents' lives, and when the music plays we find ourselves moving in much the same way, whether we want to or not. The strengths and weaknesses I see in myself seem both so Audreyish, and somehow so inevitable.

Since Dave, and our teenage Summer of Love, I was hardly ever without a man at my side, and in times of need I always looked around, as Audrey did, for a man to take care of me. I remember, in my early twenties, being in my New York apartment, in which I'd sprayed everything gold, including my boots. I sat among the gilded packing cases

I used for tables, and realized that a crisis had finally struck and my money was all gone. Nearby was a lesbian cocktail lounge where for some weeks the owner had paid me in under-the-counter cash to wear a tight leather dress and chat up customers, until she panicked about my being an illegal immigrant and let me go. I was now completely broke, but I was still too in love with Manhattan to leave. It was the city that Audrey, in her own way, had conquered. Well, so could I, and besides I wanted some good stories to take home.

I began to pick up men each night outside my favourite restaurant, the opulent Russian Tea Room, and ask them sweetly to buy me dinner. I tried to see this as my *Breakfast at Tiffany's* moment, rather than my Audrey moment, and I would even ask bemused businessmen for money 'for the powder room' as Capote's heroine Holly Golightly had done, but I soon began to feel haunted. There was too strong an echo coming down the years, and it frightened me.

Like Audrey, my restless spirit was always greedy for more, and I couldn't shake the feeling that I was searching for something – I just didn't know what that something might be. The 'Divine Discontent' seemed to be my inheritance. After America I spent several months travelling alone in India, as the fortune teller all those years ago had predicted, living in a houseboat in Kashmir, crossing the Pakistani desert on a camel and trekking through the Himalayas. I lived for a year in Spain. I would scribble long accounts of my travels to send to Audrey, perhaps hoping to outdo her with my own, more intrepid escapades.

But then I'd gone home, and it was perhaps down to Peter's presence, and that vision of their happy marriage, that I was eventually able to settle down and sustain a family life.

Sadly, Peter died of a heart attack soon before my first baby, Anna, was born. His love affair with my mother had continued for over twenty years and they'd seemed only to become happier as time went by. In the months following his death it was painful to see quite how lost Audrey was.

I missed him terribly too. For years I kept a jumper of his and would secretly smell it, to conjure that rush of warm feelings, of safety and tenderness, that he'd woken in me. I'd remember funny things – the northern way he said 'chuffed' and the comedy routine he did with his glasses mimicking his beloved Eric Morecambe, and most of all that patient kindness of his, powerful enough to move even an angry teenager. He had saved me in so many ways, and I had loved him very much. Now Audrey seemed torn between desperate grief for Peter, which sometimes had her howling like an animal, and the eternal impulse to begin the hunt for a new man. Life without one was still as unthinkable to her as ever, and it wasn't long before she'd gone back to her old ways.

One day she was pushing Anna in her buggy down a road not far from my house; I'd encouraged her to look after Anna while I was at work, hoping this would distract her, although she was an eccentric babysitter and Anna's nappy was usually put on the wrong way round and I suspected she had been fed on sweet tea and squashed-up chips. But

Anna seemed happy, and would crow with delight when her nana appeared in the doorway in sparkly sequined cardigan, lipstick and high heels. The two of them spent much of their time sitting in the minicab office near my house where the young cabbies, who made my mother laugh, smoked weed all day. I wondered if this cloud of marijuana smoke accounted for Anna's wonderful habit of sleeping through the night.

One day they came out of this odd tea party to see two youths in hoodies go into the next-door office in a suspiciously sneaky way. My mother peered in and saw them standing over a man who was sitting behind a desk, clearly threatening him and trying to force him to open his petty-cash box. She barged the door open with Anna's pushchair and gave them one of her most savage and blood-freezing tongue lashings. They soon shuffled out, apologizing and shamefaced. To thank her the man behind the desk offered to buy her lunch and from that moment on they became inseparable.

Franco De Rosa was a handsome and once rather successful Italian actor nearly twenty years her junior. He was charming, fun and kind, and he instantly adored Audrey, moving in with her and being a devoted partner. My mother was convinced that blazing stardom was still ahead of him and they then set about the project of his career revival with madcap delight.

The two of them would appear most days, stepping over Anna's toys and the debris of family life, usually with a story that they could hardly tell me for laughing so much. They

Franco De Rosa, 1980.

were often just back from blagging their way into a party: 'We talked to Joan Collins, she remembered Franco from when they both acted together in *The Stud*, of course.'

Or they were back from the Cannes Film Festival, where they had managed to get onto someone else's boat and stand next to Burt Reynolds. They'd stormed a screening by giving false names; the publicist had actually written down 'Her Duckiness of Southport' and then they'd followed Sean Connery up a huge staircase lined with a fanfare of trumpeters, only to be rumbled at the top and have to walk all the way down again past the trumpeters with everyone staring. They acted this out, hysterical with laughter. They had a wonderful collection of photographs of Hollywood stars looking astonished as Franco embraced them and Audrey flashed the camera.

Audrey was still collecting her own stories even at the end, stashing them away to pull out later, to astonish or amuse. And this form of sustenance has been passed on to me: the belief that a good story will get me through anything. That, and the thousand and one songs that, thanks to her, I seem to know the words to.

27

Arrival

THE TRAIN PULLS IN TO Liverpool Lime Street, and we are crossing the city centre to Exchange station for the connection north up the coast towards Southport. As a child I loved this walk through the city, with the density of people and the shouts of the newspaper sellers: '*Liverpool Echo*' was rasped out, like a horn, simply as '*ko!*', the sound mixed with the roar and clatter of the traffic. My small hand would feel warm and safe wrapped in my mother's soft, gloved hand as she guided us across the confusing junctions and we threaded our way through the hurried rush-hour pavements. Liverpool was dark then, a blackened city, the tall buildings stained with the soot from thousands of coal fires, the railways and marshalling yards, and the grit and smoke thrown up from the docks. On turning a corner, a great cylindrical tube would suddenly appear above the buildings, the brightly painted funnels of the ships, often with thick black smoke pouring out, struggling to make it up into the sky. That sky could be lowering, threatening rain from the Irish Sea to wash away any vestige of colour, but in that foggy gloom Audrey's fiery mane of hair and bright red lips would glow in a kind of defiance. I remember the thrill of being her pal, and how special she seemed, and all those heads turning to watch her go by.

We are all staying at the Prince of Wales Hotel for a few nights before and after the funeral. There is little trace of its past glory, and it now gets by on offering cheap breaks to pensioners. I look into the ballroom where I once played my Happy New Year game, and an organist is playing to some sleeping people who sit on plastic chairs.

I have left the children there, while I go to sort through some of my mother's things.

As I open the front door I have a feeling of overwhelming emptiness, of the world without her in it.

There on the table is the familiar contacts book, her old address book with its faded jungle-pattern cover, still held together with an elastic band. In it are all those names and places, those random pinpoints on the map that we would find ourselves heading off to all those years ago.

Next to it is a tape that I had given her for Christmas. On the label I've written 'Hello Audrey' and a list of which celebrities appear on it.

After my travels I'd become a film-maker, and when I met anyone well known I'd ask them to look at the camera and say something to her, and then I'd put all these moments on a tape to give to her. This one has Paul Newman on it, and I remember being at his house outside New York and telling him how Audrey had watched him play tennis all those years ago in the club in Palm Springs.

He'd asked about her life, and then did a quietly sincere piece saying, 'Hey Audrey, you sound like an amazing woman, and I send you all my respect and love.'

She'd loved that message, and played and replayed it to her friends and visitors.

On the same tape is George Clooney. We'd gone for a walk together, and I'd told him all about her and he compared her with his Aunt Rosemary, and then he did a turn for her. 'Hey,' he said, 'so it's the all-singing, dancing Queen for a Day, Miss Audrey Miller herself . . .'

She'd agreed he was handsome. 'Hmm, he has got a look of Clark Gable, but not as sexy.'

Robbie Williams was on there too, saying to me, 'What do you mean she won't know who I am?' Then he turns to greet her with: 'Hello Audrey, I'm Robbie Williams and I'm a singer! Fuck it, I'm not just a singer, I'm a fucking huge star. I mean huge, Audrey!'

'He didn't have to swear and spoil it,' she said when she watched, 'though he looks like he's rather sweet when he isn't showing off.'

There were many more, some highly inventive, as people rose to the challenge, and I'd give the tapes to my mother as gifts, my version of our old book of contacts, and she loved them. Now that her own travel adventures appeared to be over, I believed that I had to carry them on for us both and bring the stories home for our shared collection.

It was never easy to impress her. During my twenties I was presenting a Channel 4 current affairs series and Audrey would fidget through anything serious that I showed her, only brightening when I managed to report from an exotic location. I made one film about the new Family Law Reform Act and its impact on marriage, which I filmed mainly on an island in the Seychelles, to the bemusement of my colleagues. But I knew that the sight of me standing on a palm-fringed beach in a silk safari dress would impress her far more than one shot outside the Houses of Parliament. My next move, into making arts documentaries, cheered her up enormously as it meant going to more glamorous places, and fewer housing estates. In my career I've made many films, but only those involving something that glittered or that got me on the red carpet in a frock, or with a celebrity at my side, ever caught her magpie eye.

I've loved my job. In time, I would go back to all those places my mother and I had visited, seeing them through a different, grown-up lens and overlaying new memories onto my childhood ones. I would often feel disorientation, almost disbelief, as I arrived in New York or Los Angeles to find a driver waiting with a sign with my name on it, that I could be there, now, in such a different role. I would be struck again and again by that shift from childhood to adulthood, from powerlessness to power.

I saw, in time, that my own strengths as a film-maker lay mainly in finding characters and telling stories, and it was an industry in which, if my mother had been born thirty years later, she would have excelled. She would have seized all those opportunities, found the great story, persuaded people to give her the access, and told it with wit and flair. I would never have had the career I had if she hadn't taught me

Mum on holiday with Russell, her doctor and close friend.

how to crash into gateposts and rush through open doors, believing there will be something marvellous on the other side.

In just one generation there had been so much change, and however much she made of her opportunities, they were so different to mine.

In her later years when Franco had moved to Spain with her blessing, I had found her a live-in companion and carer: my namesake, Sally. Sally adored her, and my mother had finally settled into her old age in style. There was always a stream of visitors and plenty of male admirers.

I remembered that last Christmas, when she sat holding the gifts and cards that my children had made for her.

Now in her eighties, she still retained her glamour. Sally had manicured her hands beautifully as always, and in them she held this year's 'Hello Audrey' tape; she was gazing around at us all with some sort of contentment and I'd wondered what she was thinking. Perhaps that, after all the mad ups and downs, we had finally got to this place of grandchildren, and careers, and happy normality? And I had thought then, in that moment, 'Well, perhaps I have been good enough, after all.'

Time is running out and I begin to sort through the box of photographs, choosing the best for the slide show at the funeral after-party the following day.

Among the many love letters are those from Franco addressed to 'Her Duckiness of Southport' and Peter Cooper's to 'My Aud, My Love'. There are my father's, with his drawings of her as a naked angel, and photographs of him. I take in the youthful face, only thirty-two years old: so young for him to have to accept that he was dying. He looks such a boy to me now, and I realize just how much life he had missed out on, and how very painful it must have been to leave a wife and young child behind not knowing how the two of us would fare. Audrey had honoured her commitment to us both in her way, by marrying him and having their baby, and I suspect he forgave her the fact that she didn't sit at his bed-side each night, just as I now forgive her for not sitting beside mine when I was small. I've known the sweetness of reading bedtime stories to young children, and can hardly envy her the nights in hotel bars and desperate drives to motorway service stations for the solace of company.

My father, Neil.

The happiest photographs in the box, I now see, are of her and Peter Aspinall together. In those pictures she is clearly a woman in love. That long hunt we made together had been searching for the wrong thing in the wrong places, but Audrey had got there in the end. It had been a shot in the dark, chasing this shy widower. But she had kissed a frog and turned him into her prince. It changed us both in all kinds of ways.

As the years had gone by I was more able to see our rackety life together for the brilliant thing it was, and the many advantages of having had Audrey for a mother: the skills that she has passed on to me, her tools for survival, the diamonds that I found unexpectedly along the way. While I know that children appear to thrive with structure, routine and learning boundaries, I also know that a rudderless life can have its own great rewards. There was a sense of delighted wonder, of freely exploring the world and of doors being wide open to me, that has never deserted me. Beyond anything else, she showed me how to see the magic in things.

It was 2008 and we were on a family holiday and had just arrived at an airport in Greece. I was walking across the concourse when a distant memory suddenly struck me: my mother and I had been carrying our suitcases across a similar airport lobby, and in the early morning it was almost empty and therefore irresistible.

'Just look at that,' she said, spreading her hand in a sweeping gesture as if it were a stage set just for her. The terminal hall was wide, gleaming, as her bag dropped to the floor. 'I wish I had a pair of tap shoes . . .' but she was off out there anyway, laughing, clickety-clicking in an arc of twirls, the light catching her floating hair, her slight frame gliding and spinning as her shoes tapped out their own music. Now heads were turning and people slowing; stopping, smiling, and looking around for maybe a film camera and a director about to shout, 'Cut! And thank you, Ginger, that was wonderful!'

And it was wonderful; she was beautiful, and totally embarrassing.

She returned flushed and glowing with happiness. I felt small and awkward beside her, half proud and half ashamed, but completely thrilled.

It had been only a few days later, while I was still on that holiday in Greece, when her carer, Sally, phoned me, barely able to speak 'She's gone,' she told me, 'I can't believe it. I just went in and there she was.'

My mother had died in her sleep. The death certificate said it had been heart failure, and the world suddenly seemed an emptier place.

OUTSIDE THE CHURCH the group of men, among them my son Matt, prepare to heave the casket onto their shoulders: tiny Audrey in a big oak box that cost too much money. I can hear her in my head telling me it is nonsense. Someone fumbles with an old CD player and Nat King Cole starts up in the echoing Victorian church. *'Unforgettable'* booms out as the pall-bearers stagger down the aisle. The funeral home has interpreted my request for 'rose-strewn' by stapling roses onto the light oak at jaunty angles.

My children stand in assorted outfits, my son looking almost manly and the girls in things taken from my wardrobe.

My youngest, Moll, said the other day, 'I'm turning into you. I sing those random songs and say weird inappropriate things to strangers. My slippers even make the same slippy-slappy noise yours do.' No, we are all turning into Audrey,

Mum, Liverpool, 1932.

I think. Some personalities are so strong they hardly dilute; they are just reincarnating, taking over the future generations, living on like Dracula for centuries.

Today Moll looks so like Audrey in the photographs we will later flash up on a screen at the wake. The older girls and Matt all read poems. Moll makes her way to the pulpit like the star of the show: 'Nana never seemed like other grandmothers; she always seemed to me like Glinda, the Good Witch of the South. I can imagine her leaving the world in a big shiny bubble like the one in which Glinda left Oz. So, Nana, this is for you.' She then sings 'Somewhere Over the Rainbow' in her strong clear voice, pure Broadway. When she has finished, she bows her head with perfect timing, and goes to sit down. These genes are her inheritance, and in gratitude here she is helping Audrey make the right kind of exit.

The after-party is back at The Prince of Wales, the once-grand hotel that had seemed to me like the centre of the world. Now we are here again for Audrey's farewell. Her image is playing in a loop over the bar. It has been hard to choose from the big gold chocolate box in her wardrobe: the little Tapper with her cane, and then, a few inches taller, the leggy girl on Southport sands.

The coalyard is in the background of the Orange Day Parade as the little Queen of the Protestants rides on her Uncle Charlie's coal wagon in her 'Good Queen Bess' regalia, nose in the air. And there are picnic photos each year: the bus to the seaside or country, sandwiches and lemonade. The pictures show sea behind her, and she is squinting in the sun, freckled and happy and quite ready to take on the world.

Mum, Southport beach.

Afterword

I PUT OFF WRITING this book for decades. Not because anyone would have minded. My mother Audrey might have enjoyed any notoriety; but the story took time to process and I had to be grown up enough to tell it with some self-knowledge. I needed to understand the debt I had to her. This was never a story of damage, but rather the story of a series of gifts, for which I'm very grateful.

The other question with all memoirs is always 'how much is true?', and I can only say that I believe it is true except for certain names that have been changed, and the detail of certain scenes and conversations. I cannot of course remember what was said in a Hong Kong hotel lobby over fifty years ago, although I can remember much of what I felt at the time. I also have little evidence for dates, as there are only photographs, which are undated, and a handful of letters and mementoes, so I have sometimes had to guess and tried to be as accurate as possible. The only exception is around the making of the Norman Wisdom film which was in fact two years after Audrey's marriage to Peter. The accurate version left a rather dull couple of years between their marriage and my pre-teen rebellion, looking for hippies and boyfriends, so I left the events as they were in my memory rather than making them chronologically correct. Once I turned twelve our story became eventful once again, and so from then on I continued to be as factually correct as my memory allowed.

I've sprinkled throughout the book the usual caveats: that much is taken from the stories my mother endlessly retold; and that as a player in those stories I was aware that the events she recounted had been polished or embellished here and there. Probably I have since done this myself, in telling my own versions. But my mother's embellishments were flourishes, and the substance was true. She attracted unusual people and events to her, and she made things happen.

Fascinatingly, whenever I have been able to check out these stories the truth has often been stranger. On a visit to Southport a year or so before she died, I was invited to dinner by an old friend of my mother's and a man was there, one of the biggest property developers in the North West. We were introduced and he did a double take when he discovered who my mother was.

'Wow, you're Audrey Miller's daughter! She was an amazing character. I could tell you some stories, but I won't!'

I, of course, persuaded him that it was fine to tell all and that nothing would shock me anyway.

He began: 'The first time I met your mother was at the bar of a fancy hotel in Liverpool. I was in my twenties, and I was having a drink with a mate of mine, a good-looking guy, a footballer. Your mum came over and offered to buy us a drink. Then she said, "I don't know if you would be interested, but I know some very attractive older ladies who would pay well for the company of young men like you. And you might even have fun!"'

I asked if he had taken up her offer? He laughed and said that they hadn't, but they had been intrigued, and a few of their friends had asked them for my mother's phone number.

This only confirmed what I had always half known. At her funeral, her younger cousin Norma said to me, 'When I was young we all wondered if she was making up half of the stories that she told us; then, when I came to Southport and she introduced me to Clark Gable and he put an arm around her, I decided it was probably all true.' That was my experience of her life before I was born. It all checked out whenever I talked to anyone who had been there.

Perhaps one reason why I took so long to write this book was that for much of my life I felt overshadowed by my mother. I felt that I was the less interesting half of that funny double act of my childhood; and as the story became more mine and less hers, I wasn't sure where to stop. My antics as a teenager in Oxford seem pretty common for kids in the Seventies, and my career as a documentary maker may have some juicy anecdotes, but emotionally I was quite a settled person. As de Montherlant wrote, 'Happiness writes in white ink on a white page,' so none of this made my life as interesting as the blacker ink of Audrey's more troubled years.

However, I do believe that a harum-scarum life is no bad thing for a child. Having nothing to do, and a few books, will supply most of what we need for a vivid imaginative life and interesting self-education. I also should dedicate this book to Peter, and to all those mentors and role models out there, people who care about us even for a short time and change our lives.

Acknowledgements

First of all, a massive thank you to Dbc Pierre who said 'You *must* write this story' and then proceeded to guide me on every step of the journey with his characteristic generosity and brilliance. Thank you, too, to Jane Rogers at Gold Dust for getting me off to a good start, and to Polly Morland for all her encouragement and help.

I'm immensely grateful to Liz Wyse and Fiona Murphy, my dear friends who patiently and unwaveringly read and reread, keeping me on track with the writing, much as they do in life. To Juliet Annan, who gave me her sage guidance, to Jim Barton, Marian Macgowan, Rosemary Hill and Anne Elletson, all of whom did so much to help shape this book, and to Molly Eagles for her insightful notes, thank you so much.

My wonderful agent Patrick Walsh has supported me generously each step of the way. My editor, Helen Garnons-Williams, has offered enthusiasm, insight and nurturing throughout, and the whole team at HarperCollins have looked after me so well. Finally to my children, Anna, Meg,

Matt and Molly, for all their excellent notes, support and encouragement, a very big thank you; and to my darling Robbie who helped me in every way possible, from brilliant suggestions to pedantic fact checking and his daily unwavering support.